Acclaim

Sand Play fo

. . . Sand Play for the Soul is destined to become a classic resource in the field of human growth and spiritual development. This book reveals the power available to us when we open a personal dialogue with the Soul. The author clearly and concisely shows how we can access this power and apply it in our daily lives. The material presented is engaging and evocative. I would consider it a very great privilege and an experience of a lifetime to encounter first hand the magic of Paula Petrovic's work.

Fred Mathews PH.D.,
Author and Lecturer on Transformational Change

This book is warm, accessible to everyone, and is written in such a way as to inspire each person to become more than s/he thinks possible. Paula captures the true essence of sandplay in the powerful stories she tells of sessions she has conducted. Her grasp of the subject is remarkable. She shows how imaginative play in the sand can miraculously connect us not only to our mind and emotions but also to our soul. Hidden answers and wisdoms are released to the creator of the scene in the tray.

What makes this book truly unique is that Paula has moved sandplay one step further than it has been traditionally taken. She reveals the secret of how each individual can use this tool for themselves to answer inner questions and promote personal growth.

E. Anna Goodwin M.S., N.C.C.P, Co-author of
*Sandplay Therapy: A Step by Step Manual for
Psychotherapists of Diverse Orientations*

Sand Play for the Soul is destined to become a classic of the new-generation, self-help literature now emerging. Engagingly self-empowering, Paula's book reveals her mastery of sand play therapy and also invites the readers to discover their own soul's true voice. I strongly recommend this book both to therapists and to all who seek a brighter personal and planetary future.

Chet B. Snow, Ph.D.,
author of *Mass Dreams of the Future.*

I whole-heartedly recommend *Sand Play for the Soul* for anyone who is open to personal and professional growth, or experiencing a life transition. Paula's book captured my attention immediately and kept me fully engaged. She compassionately shares her clients' inspiring stories. Their journeys revealed profound insights that touched me deeply. Her book encourages individuals with practical specifics on how to resolve core life issues quickly and easily. Consequently, I personally have been inspired to use this unique process to address my own life challenges!

Paula's style of Sand Play is a wonderful tool for addressing the human condition in a safe and supportive manner. Furthermore, we are invited to witness creative problem-solving at its most potent when people commune with their intuition—or in Paula's words the "knowing place." *Sand Play for the Soul* is a must read for those seeking to continue evolving in consciousness in a positive and empowering way!

Tania Bloch, M.A. Co-author of the children's
picture book, *How Butterbees Came to Bee!*

I dedicate this book to my family, friends, colleagues, and participants who embarked on a Sand Play for the Soul Adventure. You dared to venture beyond limitation into New Worlds of Possibility. I have had the great fortune to journey with "the best in you" in the sandbox.

With Everlasting Thanks,

– Paula Petrovic –

Acknowledgments

First and foremost I want to express my deepest appreciation and gratitude for my family: My father, mother, and sister for surviving against extreme odds and teaching me about the power of the human spirit. You dared to defy impossible obstacles and never gave up the good fight. With the same strength of will and tenacity you have loved and believed in me.

Dear Lorna, my editor. . .one of the best decisions I have made as a writer is asking you to be on my team. Some of the greatest accomplishments in life are a result of having great people to work with.

Jim Dell, my ex-husband, dear friend and soul brother, it was your belief in my work and financial sponsorship that helped me birth SandWorks® and Sandplay Explorations®. For years you encouraged me to write this book. Here it is my dear friend. PS: It's true Ex's can make the greatest of friends.

Terry, my soul sister, our friendship is sacred. Thank you for all your love and support. We have embarked on many colorful and amazing adventures together.

Jamie, I am forever grateful for your support, guidance, and expertise in the Literary field. Your caring approach helped me step into a strange, new world with healthy awareness and confidence.

Finally, all my friends, relatives, colleagues, and the sand play participants who have been in my sand tray. Every exchange I have had with you, every Sand Play journey I have facilitated has deeply touched my life in enriching and meaningful ways. This especially includes you Tania.

Reverend Marion, (name altered to respect privacy), you top the list of my gratitude. Our story, "It's About Love, Not Fear," is in the Sand Play Stories section of this book. To this day, I do not know how the "happy face" mysteriously appeared in the text of this story. It re-enforces my knowing there is "far more to life than meets the human eye."

Table of Contents

Table of Contents

Introduction

Never in a million years could I imagine that individually selected miniatures placed in a tray filled with sand would transform people's lives so powerfully in less than ninety minutes. Fifteen years and thousands of Sand Play journeys later I continue to be in awe by what unfolds for the participants I facilitate during their adventures in the sand tray. I must confess that even after all this time I still ask myself, "how is it possible?" Who would ever think that placing some miniatures in a box of sand, along with a few simple directions, could so easily transform people's lives in such a profound manner? After several years of doing Sand Play I now find myself asking, "How can I let the general public in on the secret of Sand Play so they can make use of this life-altering tool to benefit their own lives in deep and meaningful ways?"

Whether it is a child doing battle with inner monsters causing his night terrors; a top executive of a large corporation seeking to resolve critical life issues creating undue stress; or a doctor who finds a way to put his cancer to sleep which allows him to live a vital and full life; you are about discover an awesome process for tapping into an innate resource that is limitless in what it can offer.

No matter who or where you are in the scheme of life there is a *knowing place* within your psyche that is privy to information capable of re-creating your life in extraordinary and wonderful ways. **One of the simplest means of expression known to humankind, "playing in the sand," can awaken a knowing within you with the power to create your ultimate success story!** This book invites you to learn how you can awaken this inner knowing when answers to important questions arise and need to be answered.

Envision granting yourself an opportunity to create a three-dimensional reality with your own hands simply by placing a few items in a sand tray and creating a scene. Then discovering that what you created contains information so revealing and so empowering that no issue, obstacle

When the Soul speaks and we listen, all becomes possible. Answers come quickly and easily with a clarity and truth nothing else can match.

or challenge in life can hold you back from accomplishing whatever the "highest and best in you" desires. Imagine also uncovering innate abilities that when accessed, all fears and self-doubt tainting your observations, clouding your judgments, and denying you rightful success are quickly and easily resolved. . .and all this is happening in the midst of insightful, playful fun led by a wise and resourceful ally.

This book brings to light an immense power available to you through the powerful medium of Sand Play. By following a few simple and practical guidelines you find out how to gain entrance to a *know-ing place* of infinite resource and intelligence.

When the **Soul** speaks and we listen, all becomes possible. Answers come quickly and easily with a clarity and truth nothing else can match. This has been my experience facilitating thousands of people of all ages, from all walks of life, in the sand tray. To partici-pate in and witness our stories from the *knowing place* of the Soul in concrete, tangible form opens doors to information and wisdom beyond what we commonly believe is within our reach. You discover just how empowering and limitless the *knowing place* of the Soul is when *it's* allowed to speak, and is heard.

Throughout the book you meet people from different age groups and diverse life backgrounds, playing in the sand tray having fun, learn-ing and growing in ways that exceed even their expectation of possi-bility. The Sand Play Stories tell of remarkable people facing excep-tional life challenges whose incredible journeys in the sand tray takes them back to a place of wholeness, happiness, and heartfelt purpose—once thought lost and beyond reach. Also covered in this book is the history of Sand Play as a therapeutic medium; my personal journey with *Sand Play for the Soul*; the many uses of this communication tool in everyday life; and alternative approaches to doing Sand Play.

In the last section of this book you learn how you too can go on similar Sand Play Adventures, or variations of, complementary to your needs and lifestyle. I walk you through the journey step-by-step, so you too can experience this insightful and playful process in the comforts of your own home. Logistics, facilitating your own Sand Play journey, what to do with what unfolds, and how to incorporate it into your daily life, is presented in a simple and practical manner.

Whether it is in your own home, at work, in the community, or at my studio. . .there are no limits to the creation and growth you can achieve in life when you allow yourself to be led by the *knowing place* of the Soul, especially when you use Sand Play as a vehicle for higher communication.

Author's Disclaimer and Intent

Sand Play for the Soul is not intended in any shape or form to replace psychotherapy or treatment of emotional and behavioral disturbances that may require medical or psychological treatment. Neither is this book intended to teach a person to practice psychotherapy on themselves or another. Though I have worked in the human services and mental health care fields for over twenty-seven years, I consider myself to be a facilitator, consultant, counselor and educator, not a psychotherapist. My formal education and work experience includes in-depth training in social and behavioral sciences; individual, family and childcare counseling; experiential and expressive art therapies; program development and administration; the performing arts; psychology, humanities and other areas of study. The focus of my work and style of counseling is different from many traditional approaches employed in the mental health and social services fields. The approaches I utilize in my private practice and counseling work are not better—they are simply different.

*Please note: the names of the clients, and the places they live, have been changed to respect privacy and honor confidentiality

. . .unless otherwise specified with their full agreement. Those people who wrote the testimonials, included in this book, have written them willingly and freely. I have not altered their names or the content.

*The words "sand play" in reference to it as a therapeutic process is often written as one word "sandplay" by professionals, and not always capitalized when used in such context. When quoting another's material in this book I spell it as they do. When I refer to Sand Play I spell it as two separate words and I always use capitals (Sand Play). It's a personal choice I prefer to use.

Intent:

Sand Play for the Soul is intended to offer you an opportunity to go on a fun-filled, insightful, and meaningful adventure. The information you receive and the discoveries you make have the potential to take you to places of awareness and realization that open doors to knowledge, resolution, and possibility well beyond what you may believe is within reach.

My main intent for writing *Sand Play for the Soul* is to share the gift of Sand Play and what it can offer. I have been most fortunate to witness my clients having countless discoveries and breakthroughs resulting from their sand tray creations, both in my studio, and in a variety of other settings while traveling with this work outside the studio. I want to honor and pay homage to all those who have and will embark on this incredible journey.

It takes great courage for clients to leap into the unknown and courageously walk through their darkest moments of challenge—

_____

For more in depth information on Sand Play as a clinical therapy see the "Recommended Reading" section at the end of this book.

especially when it feels like there is no hope for resolution and heal-ing. But somehow they manage to step beyond their fears, restricting belief systems, and challenging histories, to discover the full story of their lives. They find the strength to make different choices with the information they receive. These are the daring and brave ones who choose to seek out and discover the truth. They alter their lives permanently for the better by making healthier choices. These are the people who I'm continually blessed to meet and facilitate in my sand-box.

The People Who Do Sand Play Sessions with Me

The people who seek me out are looking to expand their internal resources so they can find the place within themselves where they have the power to successfully create meaning, purpose and happiness in their lives. The information they receive offers them a means of clearing mental/emotional blocks and resolving those conflicts which hold them back from successfully accomplishing their goals. The discoveries they make and information they receive from their sand tray creations through the facilitation process offers them the insight and knowledge necessary to succeed.

Often emotional and/or mental wounds, restricting belief systems and lack of self worth interfere with the desire to live healthy, happy, and wholesome lives. In these situations, I assist clients to work through and clear obstacles which prevent them from accomplishing their desired goals. In several instances their sand tray scene reveals information that helps them to have more in-depth perspective and understanding of their issues. For example, when I work with children in a therapeutic capacity, utilizing Sand Play and other experiential techniques, the parents often receive information which helps them better understand their children. Parents learn to identify and address concerns. Children also learn a lot about themselves. For young people, playing in the sandbox is non-threatening and their learning takes place naturally and easily.

Frequently a person's sand tray creation affirms what he or she already knows. What is revealed to them expands their understandings further. What they learn during the facilitation process allows them to receive feedback in a clear, concise and tangible form.

What on Earth Is Sand Play?

- Part 1 -

You are led
through your lifetime
by inner learning creatures
the playful spiritual being that is your self.
Don't turn away from possible futures
before you are certain
you don't have anything to learn from them.
Learning is finding out what you already know.
Doing is demonstrating that you know it.
Teaching is reminding others
they know as well as you.
You are all learners, doers, teachers. . .

What the caterpillar calls the end of life,
the master calls a butterfly.

Illusions
- Richard Bach -

What you may think is childish play for the
young may in fact contain THE ANSWER
capable of creating paradise on earth. Do you
dare chance missing the opportunity to
meet and co-create with the Creator
of Great and Wonderful Worlds?

- Paula Petrovic, the Sand Play Lady -

A Sand Play Story:

I'm Tired of Being in My Prescribed Little Box

Matt, a successful top executive in a large company, in his late forties, came to Sedona from out of state in hope of addressing some areas in his life that were causing him much stress. He was referred by a person who organized his week long customized retreat. He knew nothing about Sand Play beforehand.

When Matt first entered the studio, a tremendous look of surprise painted itself on his face. This high-powered executive had no idea the session involved playing in a sandbox. Once he realized what we were about to do, he just stared at me in absolute disbelief. As I did my welcoming introduction, I relied on humor in hope of preventing Matt from heading straight for and out the door. (After the session Matt confessed that his initial reaction was, "There is no way a man of my stature and disposition is going to play in the sandbox. This is totally silly and a waste of time.") Fortunately for both of us I said the right words and he decided to stay.

Once Matt got over his initial shock of what he was about to do, he noticed an extensive collection of miniatures representing our everyday three-dimensional world (items from the human, earth, animal and spiritual kingdoms) sitting on the shelves lined up along the walls. Feeling more at ease and open to the journey he was about to embark on, Matt's attitude about doing Sand Play quickly shifted. His eyes lit up like a kid in a candy shop and suddenly he couldn't wait to begin the journey. We did a clearing to calm his mind of busy thoughts, and set the intent for the session, so that the *knowing place*—the place that has all the answers—would help guide the way during the creation and facilitation of his sand tray scene. Curious and ready to go on a sand play adventure, he scanned the shelves, collected a variety of miniatures, and quickly created his tray scene. He could hardly wait to explore the significance of his sand tray scene and why he had picked the items he did for his creation. The intrigue of discovery had eagerly taken hold of his psyche. This is a condensed version of his session. . .

Paula: As you observe the world you created what is your first impression?

Matt: Lots of stuff is cluttered in the area I put my house. There are different separations and themes in my tray scene. I'm surprised I didn't integrate the separate pieces in my tray in a cohesive fashion. . .the religious figures. . .I don't know why I picked them.

Paula: We will explore the significance of these figures shortly. Did any feelings come up as you observed the world you created?

Matt: It's reflective of how I feel. There's a variety of stuff. It's funny. . .the people and things I put there. . .they are all representative of how I feel. The religious figures are next to my home. The warriors on the periphery are

doing battle. The troll situated on the other side represents the band I played in years ago. I haven't played in
one since.

Paula: I'm curious about the guy in the center of your tray.

Matt: I am too. It feels like Wisdom and he's in charge.

Paula: What does the man in charge have to say?

Matt: He's in charge.

Paula: In charge of what?

Matt: (Deep emotions surface.) Why am I so emotional?

I encourage Matt to be present with his emotions and allow whatever wants to surface to arise.

Matt: This is me.

Paula: When you say it's you, where do you feel that response
in your body?

Matt: In my gut. It feels brokenhearted. It feels sad. (Matt
cries as he says this.)

The wisdom part hurts. I feel tired of being the wise person and
always the strong one.

Paula: What does wisdom want you to know about your life?

Matt: FUN! Fun is missing in my life and it's affected me
deeply in a sad way. (Matt is profoundly affected by this

realization.). . .Look here. . .the warriors. . .they feel separated from one another – not part of a group. . .it's pieces of me feeling fragmented...

Matt and I talked about how people and situations in our life reflect back to us what we need to know. Then we talked about the lady in his life.

Matt: She's that spontaneity I do not have. I've been too seri- ous and analytical. I feel lighter and freer when I'm around her. I have always been so serious. During my childhood I had to be responsible. There was little room for laughter and play. I had to grow up fast to do what was expected of me. My sand tray scene is deeply affecting me. I was aware of my seriousness but now I'm seeing and experiencing it at a different level. I can feel how it holds me back from being free and sponta- neous with my actions. There is no room for fun when I'm like this. I want to release this intense and serious part of me. It does not allow me to be happy.

Paula: Ask the wisdom part how to do this. What does he say?

Matt: Bessie comes to mind (Matt's girlfriend). . .I'm stuck now.

I sense that Matt's wise part is equated with seriousness and lots of responsibility and he is not yet able to allow Wisdom to reveal its true identity. I sense he needs a strong ally to get unstuck. Often I rely on close observation and instinct when facilitating a client. . .how and what he says. . .his tone of voice, body language, information offered or not. . .to assist in seeing where to go next in the session. There is often much more going on than what appears to be happening on the surface.

Paula: If it is okay with you, let's explore the warriors.

Matt: (He nods.) They're knights in shining armor. They have the ability to come to the rescue. That's me trying to rescue every one else. And the superman figure standing next to them DOES THE SAME THING.

Matt is fed up and tired of always being the one to rescue and "save the day." The expression in his voice clearly reflects this. I notice Matt looking intently at a figure standing in his sand tray near the warriors.

Paula: What's his story?

Matt: That's Spock*. He represents an intelligent person who's not emotional. He does what needs to be done. I wish I were more like him. (*Spock is a character from the Star Trek television series created by Gene Roddenberry.)

Paula: What would he say about having fun?

Matt: Do it!

Paula: I suggest you do something fun everyday.

Matt: Why does that not feel good to hear?

I ask Matt to get a figure that represents the fun part of him and put it next to the figure he refers to as the "one in charge" (Wisdom/the Wiseman.)

> Matt: You had me worried there for a minute. I thought you were going to ask me to remove my Wise Person.

I assure Matt that the Wise Person is a crucial part of his life that wants to help him expand who he is. Having fun is a foreign idea to Matt even though he very much wants to allow himself to experience more of it. Being wise and having fun does not quite blend well together for him just yet. I want to provide Matt with the opportunity to allow the wise part of him, which also happens to be intelligent, capable and resourceful, to help him explore what it would be like to have fun. In watching Matt earlier, he appeared to very much enjoy selecting his miniatures and creating his tray scene. He was definitely enjoying himself and he couldn't wait to begin the facilitation. FUN had already entered his world in a big way yet he did not fully realize or grasp what that really meant.

Matt puts the cartoon character known as Gumby (a friendly, bendable, green figure designed by Art Clokey) behind the Wise Person and little off to the side to represent fun. He then talks about not being able to let Gumby stand right next to the Wise Person. I tell Matt, "Baby steps. . .just take one step at a time. It's important to allow yourself time to adjust to introducing fun into your life." Matt had a difficult childhood. Being capable, wise and responsible kept him safe and able to function reasonably well during this trying period. I reminded him of something he had said earlier. "Matt, you said Bessie represents the qualities of spontaneity and fun and this is what you love about her. Perhaps the Wisdom in you would like you to allow for fun and spontaneity in your life so this part of you can grow and expand in a more fulfilling way."

> Matt: I am becoming more aware of the need to open up those parts of myself. The message in my scene is very clear.

Matt talks about his previous failed marriage and how he's afraid he will lose Bessie because he is so serious and intense. He talks in some depth about how his survival during childhood depended on being strong to take care of the family. He grew up fast and never really learnt how to play and have fun. Until now he understood this only on an intellectual level; however, he had not understood the physical and emotional impact the lack of childhood play had on his adult relationships. Matt was very surprised that he could cry and feel as much as he did viewing his tray scene. He said this felt very freeing.

I told Matt, "What you didn't receive or get to do as a child you can give and do for yourself today. And that's something you can then pass on to your children." (Matt speaks about how he felt disconnected from his children from his previous marriage. He says he really wanted to be closer to them in a freeing, less intense manner.)

> Matt: Paula, I'm so tired of being in my little prescribed box. This is bigger than even Bessie. As much as I love her and want to save the relationship, I want to enjoy life and have fun, without having to rely on Bessie to show me the way. I want to be spontaneous and free to be all I can because of me—not because of someone else.

> Paula: Matt don't forget about your music.

Matt played in a band for years and enjoyed it very much, yet he had stopped playing and couldn't remember why.

Paula: Explore your love of music and allow yourself to have fun without an agenda. Let the child part see there's more to life than you believed there could be when you were little.

Matt was surprised so much could be revealed to him in just one session by simply playing in the sand. He felt as if a huge weight had been lifted off his shoulders. Doing the healing retreat in Sedona was not about saving his relationship with Bessie, it was about saving himself.

Power of Sand Play

The image that usually comes to mind when I try to explain what Sand Play is to others is a line from a song in the movie "Mary Poppins," "A teaspoon of sugar makes the medicine go down". . .though in my mind I always hear the word "help" the medicine go down. Having fun creating a sand tray scene and receiving vital, meaningful information in such a simple, playful manner makes serious issues that need to be addressed and resolved a lot easier to digest. Pivotal, life-transforming information is revealed with great ease, depth and accuracy. Seeking creative solutions to core problems that hold us back from accomplishing our life goals has tremendous benefit, especially when answers come to us with unwavering clarity.

Much in our lives and belief systems can cause unnecessary pain, suffering and stress. In many instances we are unable to successfully address the pain due to lack of information about its true origin. Why not discover the complete story quickly and easily? Through the Sand Play process we gain information to help us make more informed decisions. You would be amazed how a few miniatures placed in a tray filled with sand can reveal so much. The personal accounts in this book show how revealing and empowering Sand Play is, as expressed through the eyes of the Soul.

What Is Sand Play?

Traditionally Sand Play is a means through which you are given opportunity to tell your story graphically in a sand tray. The sand tray (which may vary in size) has a blue interior to represent sky and water, and is filled with sand to symbolize earth. Using a collection of miniatures that represent the three-dimensional world we live in (i.e. rocks, plants, animals, people, buildings, household items, transport vehicles, mythical, spiritual or religious, cartoon figures, the list continues...) you select items that are symbolically important to you, either consciously or subconsciously. With the chosen items, you create a sand tray scene. What comes next is determined by the Sand Play therapist's style of working with this process.

"Sandplay provides an opportunity for the client to represent in images what is happening in a person's inner and outer world."

Typically, the practitioner notices what items take predominant positions; what comforts; what blocks; what's uplifting and what's threatening to the client in their scenes. Male figures, female figures, houses and/or commercial buildings, spiritual and/or religious symbols, wild animals and/or tame animals, items for nonsensical, practical, or symbolic use. . .so much to choose from depending on the therapist's size of collection. Every placement is meaningful in relation to the other pieces placed. Ideally the therapist observes, never inter-fering in the client's personal process. He or she listens to what the client says about the scene and asks questions where appropriate and when necessary. They assist the client to bring the tray scene symbol-ically to life in support of the therapeutic process.

My friend and colleague, E. Anna Goodwin, and her coauthor Barbara Labovitz Boik, wrote about Sand Play in their highly acclaimed book, *Sandplay Therapy: A Step-by-Step Manual for Psychotherapists of Diverse Orientation*. In it, they beautifully captured the essence of this therapeutic medium:

> "The client, using the senses of touch, sight and smell, brings into physical form her/his innermost conscious and unconscious thoughts and feelings. Sandplay, through the use of active imagination and creative symbolic play, is a practical, experiential tool that can create a bridge from the unconscious to the conscious, from the mental and the spir-itual to the physical and from the nonverbal to the verbal. Sandplay provides an opportunity for the client to represent in images what is happening in a person's inner and outer world. That is, the images become a language through which the client can communicate unconscious material to the therapist and to her/himself, resulting in greater under-standing and behavior change. It allows the client to create aspects of an entire issue with symbolic objects that can be easily touched and changed. When a therapist trusts the unconscious mind of the client to reveal its unique and perfect path to self-discovery, deep transformational work can occur for both client and therapist."

In my studio, or when I travel with my work, I set the intent for the session and facilitate the process unfolding for the client (also referred to as "participant") such that the Sand Play scene that the participant creates, comes to life through the eyes of their soul. This assists the individual to tap into his or her higher knowingness within as guided by the Soul. By utilizing all of our physical, mental, emotional and spiritual senses (known or yet to be revealed), we embark on a journey.

What Is Sand Play for the Soul?

Sand Play for the Soul takes Sand Play to another level of expression. It is an opportunity to go on a fun-filled, action-packed, soul-inspired adventure with a companion—one who does not judge, manipulate or lie to you. Instead you are supported and guided by a presence of being who always tells you the truth. . .the untainted version; the self-reflection which shows you who you "REALLY ARE" in the larger scope of your life—even when you are thinking "small" or are confined by limiting beliefs. This companion helps you to see, hear, feel and experience a knowing within you that is fully aware of what needs to be done to support and assist you to become "all you can be." This divine knowingness helps you to transcend any preconceived belief system that tries to convince you that you are unworthy, incapable and cannot succeed.

This companion is the Soul, an energy force within that knows how to do what needs to be done when you do not. There is nothing you cannot accomplish when you and your soul are in league as "One." Communicating with your soul in the three-dimensional form in the sand tray is a surprising, eventful journey loaded with twists and turns of every imaginable variety. . .and those yet to be imagined. . .all leading to one ultimate destination: The whole truth and nothing but the truth of who you are in the bigger picture of your life.

Sand Play through the Eyes of the Soul

The following information reflects a typical journey participants experience when they embark upon a *Sand Play for the Soul* Adventure:

The studio or sacred place is quiet, inviting and safe the moment you enter. I introduce myself and engage you in welcoming, easy conversation to build rapport; I may add a touch of humor to encourage ease and help prepare you for the play experience. Then, I briefly speak about what will happen during the journey. Next, you are guided through a simple and relaxing visualization which helps to calm the mind and quiet busy thoughts. Then, we set the intent: I ask you to ask your *knowing place*, "the place that has all the answers," one question. . ."What do I need to know about my life at this time. . .show me the way?" Time and space are provided to allow for inward activation of the *knowing place*.

The sojourn of the Soul abundant with discovery, revelation and adventure is now only moments away. When you are ready, you are invited to begin selecting from a myriad of aesthetic, quality miniatures, from the spiritual and symbolic to the everyday realms of the human, animal and earth kingdom. These visually enriching reflections of our diverse physical world are there for you to create your scene. How and what you select is at your sole discretion. You are the "master creator" and the world is yours to form into being.

Once you create your scene, I facilitate you through a "Soul meets self" process which assists you to begin opening up channels of communication with your *knowing place*. Shortly into the initial link-up, I ask you to walk around your scene and look at it from different angles. Time and space is available for silent reflection. Soon the scene starts to come to life and your soul begins to reveal itself to you in meaningful and surprising ways. Once you walk full circle around the tray and experience your first impressions of your scene, the facilitation begins.

The facilitation style used and questions asked support you in a gentle and non-threatening way to dialogue with your soul's knowing-ness. As you verbalize what your Sand Play tray scene is about, you hear YOU speaking to yourself telling you what you need to know or realize. Your inner knowledge reveals itself to your outer self and what you most need to know about your life at this time is revealed.

Soon it becomes clear you are experiencing something unlike you ever experienced before. The scene feels so real and true to life. A voice inside you awakens and it feels deep and eternal. You discover, "Never before have I seen things so clear and felt so connected to something so alive and aware." The verbal, visual and sensory experiences taking place, assisted by the facilitation, allow you to view your world from a whole new perspective. Suddenly, what made no sense and seemed impossible to resolve is not so confusing or difficult. By the end of the journey your face has a huge smile which says, "Playing in the sand box was empowering and revealing. I would never have believed myself so capable and able to resolve my problems quickly and easily had I not experienced this for myself."

History of Sand Play as a Therapeutic Medium

People have been playing in the sand since the beginning of time. How sand play evolved into a therapeutic medium to help people heal their troubled psyches is fascinating. My sister, Vera Petrovic, who is a medical doctor specializing in psychiatry, was profoundly and positively affected by a Sand Play session I did with her twelve years ago. As a result of her experience, she wrote a paper for a required psychology course. With her permission, the following section comes directly from this paper entitled "Sandplay Therapy: A Healing Process," for Psyche 334 (Waterloo University, Canada), written in November, 1994.

History of Sandplay Therapy

The origin of sandplay technique can be traced to ancient times, when primitive rituals traced protective circles in the sand (Kalff, 1980, pp 24-29; Sachs, 1990).

It was Carl Jung who first formulated a clinical explanation of the therapeutic value of sandplay therapy (C.G. Jung Institute, 1981). He explained in his autobiography that playing and building villages in the sand helped him transcend the spiritual despondency he experienced as a result of his split with Freud (Kahn, 1989). Fantasy, he explained, joined together the inner and outer world (Kahn, 1989), and could reach the unconscious in a way that dreams may not be able to (Jung, 1965, p 173ff).

The actual development of the sandplay technique was accomplished by a British physician named Margaret Lowenfeld. After WWI, Lowenfeld went to Poland to help deal with the destitution and hardship caused by the war. As she watched the children adjust to their ordeals she noticed some did better than others. She noticed the ones who did better were able to express their fears by drawing in the sand. During this time she discovered she could reach the unreachable minds of children in refugee camps by using objects, toys and sand. Children were able to express, with play, what they had been unable to express with language. This led Dr. Lowenfeld to conclude that verbal communication was an inadequate medium for expressing crucial aspects of the human experience, thoughts, feelings, sensations, concepts and memories (Lowenfeld, 1979, pp 2-4).

Shaped by these experiences, Dr. Lowenfeld decided to enter the field of psychotherapy, with particular emphasis on children and the study of their emotionality. At the time this was a growing field of interest and one which needed much developing. Dr. Lowenfeld believed that the key to understanding the minds of children was through toys and play. In 1928, she opened a clinic for nervous and difficult children. The clinic contained some toys – building bricks, plasticine, colored paper, stencils, dolls and a bowl of water with rubber toys in it.

In 1929, Margaret Lowenfeld created "The World Technique," a method in which sandplay was used as therapy in conjunction with other play therapies at the clinic. The method employed the use of a sand tray, water, tools and two and three dimensional figures, to help nervous and disturbed children express their ideas and feelings. They did this by creating their own worlds in the sand tray.

Margaret Lowenfeld's aim in creating the sandplay technique was twofold: to devise a method with which children can demonstrate their own emotional and mental states without intervention from an adult, and which would allow a record to be made of such a demonstration (Lowenfeld, 1979, pp 3-7).

In the 1950s, Dora Kalff, a Swiss Jungian analyst and student of Margaret Lowenfeld, realized that the World Technique was ideally suited as a creative Jungian psychotherapeutic play technique. While Dr. Lowenfeld acknowledged the value of using sandplay for adults, her focus was children. It was Dora Kalff and her students who extended sandplay as a psychotherapeutic tool for adults as well as children. Over the years, Kalff further developed the sandplay technique, formulated its theoretical principles and trained many practitioners throughout the world. (Allan & Berry, 1987; Schubach-DeDomenico, 1988, p 26-29; Kahn, 1989, p 26; Ammann, 1991, pp 1-128.").

Who Is Paula in Relation to Sand Play?

In 1991, when I first began to include Sand Play in my counseling work, I had already worked in the Human Services field for fourteen years as a child and family care counselor, project supervisor, group leader, teacher, facilitator and consultant, as well as having recently completed my master's degree. When Sand Play suddenly entered my world, I was ready to expand my personal and professional horizons. Soon this modality became a way of life. My relationship to Sand Play and how I use it in my work quickly evolved into an "inner world adventure of a lifetime."

Over several years, I have had the great fortune to discover there is so much more to the art of Sand Play than has been traditionally used in the clinical realms of psychotherapeutic practice. As a private consultant, facilitator, educator, and counselor, I have used numerous innovative and experiential therapeutic techniques including creative visualization, voice dialogue, art and drama therapies, and more. Using these techniques in my work was as easy as breathing. Adding sand tray play to my repertoire of healing tools was an easy leap to make.

What Sand Play did for my clients was far more reaching in scope than I could have ever imagined. It was the experience of creating my own tray scenes that helped me to fully know its immense power to positively transform people's lives.

One of my most memorable early experiences with Sand Play was during an exercise I was asked to do at a training program in Sand Play Therapy taught by Gisela Schubach De Domenico, Ph.D. in Oakland, California.

All that existed in my world at that moment felt simple, free and innocent. . . I felt as if I belonged to something most wonderful, loving, and crystal clear.

Gisela asked each of us in the program to place four objects in our individual trays and to allow whatever messages came from the unconscious into the conscious to do so spontaneously. What surfaced from deep within my heart, soul and psyche was absolutely profound. No experience in the sand tray since has had as deep and powerful impact on me as that one scene did, except for one other time. (The story: "Its About Love Not Fear" is in the Sand Play Stories Section.)

The four items I put in the tray were a glass pyramid with a hollow interior and open doorway; a clear quartz crystal with a slight emerald tinge; a black stone figure, ancient and primal looking; and live cedar tree tips. I placed the crystal inside the glass pyramid in the center of the tray. Outside, to the right of its doorway, stood the stone figure. I arranged the cedar tips in a circular fashion on the periphery of these two pieces. As I did this, I felt a strong surge of energy vibrate throughout my entire body. The experience initially felt very strange.

I took a deep breath of acceptance and exhaled the intense energy building inside me. I did this for about five minutes, and soon I found myself in a place of total relaxation and surrender. I kept viewing my mini scene in the tray, and its impact with a grateful heart.

Soon, I felt a deep, embracing, playful joy. It expanded inside me and was followed by immense sense of peace, ease, and well-being. All that existed in my world at that moment felt simple, free and innocent. My heart fluttered, and mist came to my eyes. In the ensuing moments I felt as if I belonged to something most wonderful, loving, and crystal clear. It was a presence unlike I had ever experienced before. The playful, embracing innocence I felt from it had no fear or doubt. It just was what it was and did not need to do or prove anything. I felt this presence ask me just to be. And that I did. . .Just Be. I queried in blissful curiosity, "Who or what are you hugging every cell of my body in such a joyful, all-loving, gentle embrace? It responded, "I am God."

Five minutes later, in the distant reaches of my mind, I heard Gisela saying it was time to move on to the next exercise. Leaving this divine bliss and returning to the workshop to do another exercise was exceptionally difficult. I wanted to be in this state forever. My resistance to move on to the next exercise was strong and unrelenting. I did not want to leave this blissful state. Then I heard a soft spoken whisper trickling through my thoughts saying, "I'll be back." Still, I did not want to let go.

During the next exercise we had to do another sand tray scene. I placed a number of items in it, including an elongated, tube-shape-stone, standing upright. Every time I diverted my attention from this current exercise to the one I just did previously, the stone would topple over, and I would hear a serene whisper in the back of my mind saying, "It's time to move on to the next experience; I'm still here, only in a different way." Eventually, I acquiesced, and returned to the task the group was being asked to do.

Jim

Prior to my first introduction to Sand Play, I moved into a funky studio space in Sedona, Arizona, that Jim—my husband at the time—intended to use for his new career building functional art made of wood. Although he was already a helicopter pilot and sailor, his newest passion was to build a beautiful cedar-strip canoe, known as the "Wee Lassie." After he completed the first and only canoe he made, he moved on to a bigger and grander endeavor: building the perfect sailing vessel to sail the high seas. My free-spirited husband no longer had use for the workshop space. However, I did have use for it, as Jim's destiny blew in another direction. He returned to Alaska to fly helicopters to earn money to pay for his new passion: building a fifty foot wooden sail boat by hand. I, on the other hand, knew that I was to remain in Sedona and live in this studio—absent of bath and kitchen facilities. I did not know why—only that something was about to happen that would change my life. . .and it most certainly did!

When Sand Play and I First Met

A short time later I met Valerie, a teacher trained in Waldorf education, while visiting Hawaii. When we met on the beautiful island of Kauai, she had recently decided to spend more time living there. Discovering that I lived in Sedona, where she had lived before, she asked if I could baby sit some boxes while she decided about permanently moving to Hawaii. When she chose later to remain there, she asked me to sort through her boxes and ship certain personal possessions to her. In the process, I found the book written by Doris Kalff called *Sandplay: A Psychotherapeutic Approach to the Psyche.* Curious, I read the introduction and was mesmerized. I did not read the rest of the book. I was too busy experimenting and testing the waters on how to utilize this therapeutic medium to explore deeper into the psyche. The same box contained a small collection of miniature figures. I asked Valerie if I could buy these from her. She agreed and the beginnings of my miniature collection for Sand Play found its way into my studio. My collection grew quickly and continued to do so for many years.

Jim, who had since returned from flying helicopters in Alaska, built me a sand tray, some shelves and then whole-heartedly decided to financially sponsor my work, even years after we peacefully and amicably parted ways to pursue separate dreams.

First Clients

Among the first few clients to enter my studio were five year old Jason suffering from night terrors; BJ, a woman in her late thirties who was trying to stop smoking; and an eight old Tibetan/American boy named Sung, whose mother was faced with a crucial, life-altering decision concerning her son. In working with them, I was made privy to an amazing process which would take my personal and professional life to new heights of exploration, discovery and realization. I fell totally in love with the magical process of Sand Play. My experiences working with these three people allowed my work to move to a new level of evolution. Here are their stories. . .

Jason and the Two Lizards

One day I received a phone call from a desperate mom. She was afraid her five-year-old son, Jason, was about to have a mental, emotional, and physical breakdown. For four years he had not been able to sleep through the night. Horrifying nightmares kept him awake for large portions of the night. Shortly after Jason fell asleep he'd wake up screaming. It took his mother hours to calm him down before he was able to fall back to sleep. His mother was beside herself with worry and tried everything she knew to help her son feel safe and secure in hope of helping him sleep. She herself had faced a health challenge that caused her to be bedridden for a few years starting when Jason was a year old. On a number of occasions the boy's father had to step in to assist his wife, yet even that was not enough. With two other children to take care of as well, neither mother nor son was doing well when they first came to my studio.

Anyone who has been severely sleep-deprived knows how challenging it can be to operate effectively day-to-day. After four years of interrupted sleep, Jason and his mom were barely able to function in their daily routines. Going shopping, playing in the park and other daily activities often took more energy than they had in their weakened conditions.

The first time Jason came through my studio door he saw the collection of miniatures on the shelves and the sand tray in the center of the room. He immediately went to work creating his scene. Initially, there was minimal dialogue between us. Jason was on a mission and much too busy to talk. It was just he, the tray, and the miniature world he was building in the sand. As he checked out the numerous miniatures on the shelves, a lizard sitting on a rock caught his attention. His eyes instantly lit up. He immediately placed the lizard in the tray. Then he added a replica of the USS Constitution sailing vessel and several mean-looking warriors to do battle. Soon the scene was complete. Jason spontaneously began to play with the figures in the sand and the battle raged on. The mean warriors were out to kill the lizard by whatever method possible. The lizard fought back fiercely. No matter how the warriors came after him, the lizard found a way to defend himself. Sometimes the mean warriors ended up dead but they always came back to life. As the battle continued, lizard versus warriors, the lizard hung on and refused to be killed. I asked Jason who the lizard was and he said "His name is Jason." As the session drew to an end the boy commented as he walked out the door, "Miss Paula, the battle is not yet over; there is more fighting to do."

The next day the mother called me and said her son had slept through the entire night for the first time in four years. Jason came to see me a few days later and continued where he left off using the same figures he had in the previous session. This time he discovered I had another lizard identical to the one he had used in the first session. (The day before I had a feeling I needed to buy another lizard just like the one Jason used, and had done so.) The young boy had a huge smile on his face when he saw the second lizard. He quickly grabbed it and placed it in the tray next to the other lizard. He named the lizards Jason 1 and Jason 2, both of whom fought the mean warriors without retreat. This time the mean warriors began to die and were not able to come back to life to attack the lizards as they had done in his scene a few days earlier.

Jason came for four more sessions. His mother told me that by the fourth session he was drawing pictures of the monsters that had been terrorizing him in his dreams. In the pictures he and the monsters became friends and they no longer wanted to harm him. His sleep patterns became normal and he was able to sleep through the night, rarely having bad dreams. Five years later he joined a Community Building Sand Play Workshop I was facilitating for children. He was no longer a timid boy haunted by terrifying monsters. Jason became a leader who liked to take charge, so much so he had a tendency to dominate the group, always wanting to be the center of attention and to have things be the way he wanted them to be. Learning to tame this newly acquired assertiveness was a challenge for Jason. However, by the sixth week of the workshop series he learned to listen, be receptive to the needs of others, and lead by invitation rather than domination, as he navigated his peers on a Sand Play Adventure. The children looked up to him and thoroughly enjoyed the stories he told. As I followed his progress, I learned that in his early teens he developed a love for playing electrical guitar and demonstrated a natural talent for the instrument. The last I heard he was being scouted by a talent agent.

Commentary: When Jason was a year old his mother had contracted the disease, Lupus. Soon into the illness her health grew grave and she became very fragile. After observing the boy, and speaking with his mother at length about her medical history, I felt certain that the monsters in the child's dreams were a reflection of his mother's disease. His perceptions of his mother's illness had found a home in Jason's psyche. When his mom first came to me to seek help for her son, the Lupus disease had lost most of its hold over her and her health had dramatically improved. Jason's psyche, however, could not let go of the monsters representing his mother's disease until he battled them in the sand tray. His lizard friends, Jason 1 and Jason 2, were his means of conquering the monsters. The second lizard was a back up support to assure the victory he so badly desired and needed.

Children have a natural tendency and an amazing ability to take on the identities and experiences of their parents. It is often as if the experiences were their own. They are especially vulnerable to their mother's experi-

Children have a natural tendency and an amazing ability to take on the identities and experiences of their parents. It is often as if the experiences were their own.

ences during the early phases of childhood. In most cases the mother, who gives birth and is most often the primary caregiver during the child's early years, has the greatest influence on the baby or toddler. Children bond deeply with the caregiver who is most involved in the earliest years of their upbringing. They are like sponges–absorbing the thoughts, feelings, and perceptions of the dominant people in their lives.

Adults do not realize a child experiences much more of what going on than he or she is given credit for. At a young age children have little ability to discern what is them and what is not. Not until they are old enough to differentiate between their parents and themselves are they able to separate their own experiences from events in their parents' lives. And even then as adults, some people have not yet truly disengaged from their parent's identity.

It wasn't until Jason was five and his mother's health had dramatically improved that either of them were able to come to grips with the nightmares. The sand tray, along with the safe environment of the studio and my presence, allowed him to face those terrifying monsters head on. It was time, and the knowing self within Jason provided him the strength to face and make peace with his demons. The experience also allowed his mother to release the fears and guilt she had felt over not being there for her son in the way she had wanted to be.

In just one hour of Sand Play, Jason showed his strength and ability to marshal his forces in dealing with the monsters. During the five sessions there was minimal talking between him and myself. Simply providing the opportunity and a safe space for his battle to take place are what helped him turn the horrifying monsters into his friends. In this instance, talk therapy would almost certainly not have helped Jason. My being present, accepting and supportive of his Sand Play journey did. Through sand tray play he showed me his many sides of Self. His inner strength and innate ability to seek creative solutions to his core issues will guide him successfully through the twists and turns of life.

BJ and the Giant Cigarette

One day, a neighbor named BJ came to me and said she wanted to stop smoking. Smoking three packs a day was adversely affecting her health. She told me she had tried everything on the market designed to help a person stop smoking and nothing had worked. At the beginning of the session I helped BJ set the intent for the session: allow her smoking habit to speak to her during the Sand Play and tell her what it wanted from her. She wholeheartedly agreed and spontaneously went to work creating her scene. Selecting the miniatures from the shelves that caught her attention, she placed them in the sand tray. One item she wanted I did not have was a replica of a giant cigarette. For BJ, cigarettes had taken over her life and she felt their only intent was to kill her! She wanted the biggest one she could have to represent the destructive impact it was having on her life.

She proceeded to construct a giant cigarette from a paper towel roll and placed it in the center of her tray. Surrounding the giant cigarette were members of her family—her husband, parents and other close relatives. As I began the facilitation process, two particular figures that she had placed in a prominent position beside her giant cigarette held her attention. We began to explore the significance of those figures. Soon into the process BJ broke down in tears. Seeing these two petite figures (she identified as her parents) standing next to the giant cigarette triggered a profound sense of loss, emptiness and sadness deep within her. As the emotions connected to these feelings surfaced, BJ made a powerful discovery.

She discovered that the suckling quality of holding a cigarette to her lips soothed and brought her comfort, yet it also punished her. As a child, growing up, she never received love and affection from her parents. As a result, she always felt something was missing. In an attempt to fill the void in her life, she used cigarettes to replace what she felt was long lost to her as a child. Smoking never actually filled the emptiness yet she continued to smoke, up to three packs a day, in attempt to fill this void. Doing so triggered anger and hurt, and those also served an important role. Her emotionally unavailable parents, when they did respond, had nothing positive to say about their daughter, and they let her know it. What BJ heard was she was unworthy and not good enough. This belief carried into her adulthood. The emptiness remained and so did the lack of self worth. The cigarettes served to soothe and punish her at the same time. When the cigarettes revealed their true role to her she was shocked. Truth exposed, she found she could no longer smoke.

BJ initially came to the sand tray experience in hope of discovering why she could not stop smoking. Once she discovered how destructive and negating her habit was to her journey of self-discovery and healing—she had passionately pursued for some time—the thought of smoking disgusted her. She realized that her smoking was a deceptive vice that lied to her. This vice wanted her to believe it was serving a purpose necessary to her survival when, in fact, it was not. Over the next few months BJ discovered the truth behind her parents' behavior and realized their actions had nothing to do with her. She discovered something far better and more satisfying to replace the long-felt void resulting from her upbringing. She replaced the void with a deep desire to enjoy her family and expand her personal horizons—this became her number one priority.

Sung, the Tibetan Boy

Eight year-old Sung, who is half Tibetan and half American, was at an interesting crossroads in his young life. Sung's mother told me her son was restless and upset and she did not know why. The mother suspected it might be because a Buddhist sect in Bhutan wanted to take him to be raised in their monastery. They had told her Sung was a reincarnation of the first companion to a deceased spiritual Lama who had recently returned in body form. This spiritual leader would one day become an important Lama who would do great service for the world. Sung, being his first companion, would serve a crucial role in this Lama's life. Sung's mother had many concerns and reservations about allowing her son to leave her at such an early age. She was not sure this would be a wise choice. Her son, upon being approached by this Buddhist sect, started to display behavioral problems at home.

The moment Sung walked through the door of my studio during his first session he immediately approached the tray to create his scene. Without being told, he knew exactly what to do. When he had finished laying out his scene, he proceeded to tell me with great eagerness and trust about alternate realities, time-line events happening in simultaneous worlds, and reincarnation. He seemed completely comfortable and at ease sharing his stories. Over the next three months he continued to tell me these stories on a consistent basis. The wisdom and information revealed through his sand tray scenes held me spell-bound and he told me it was to be our secret. One day he would share with others when they were ready to listen. At the end of three months his mother said Sung had become significantly calmer and seemed more at peace within himself.

The last time I saw Sung he had sadness in his eyes. It was to be the last time he would create his scenes in my sand tray and share his stories with me. He told me he and his mom had to move away and our journey together would be over. Sung told me he wanted me to have his special rock collection as a tribute in appreciation for the work we had done together. His rock collection was indeed special and unusual. The stones remain in my studio to this day and have blessed many sand tray creations with their beauty and power. I still feel Sung's presence in the rocks.

A Sand Tray Scene Never Lies

Five years after I began facilitating Sand Play sessions in my studio, I had successfully merged being a consultant, facilitator, educator, and therapist with the amazing communication medium of Sand Play. As I mastered my trade, growing personally and professionally, the more in awe I became by what unfolded for clients during their Sand Play sessions. The wonderful effect it had on my clients continued to hold merit; no tray was ever ugly, boring or absent of meaning. Each and every sand tray scene created was beautiful, revealing, and always told the truth. Even when a client appeared to be initially unresponsive to the Sand Play experience, the seed of awareness was planted in the person's psyche. Sometimes the effects took a few weeks, a few months and on the rare occasion a couple of years to translate and integrate fully into the client's lives. When the integration took place, clients reported the resulting effect as being wondrous, fulfilling and heartwarming. Once the person was ready, much to their great and pleasant surprise, they received the gift the sand tray had for them.

The smallest recognitions can transform a life in deep and meaningful ways.

In one session a client named John, age 60 and retired due to wise investments, said he hated doing Sand Play. I was surprised at hearing this. My recollection of his session was of a man who was full of stories yearning to be told. Through the grapevine I heard he began writing prose which was beautiful and eloquently written. At one point, I was fortunate to hear some of those stories. His negative response to Sand Play was an unsolved mystery. Ultimately, a year and a half later, he wrote informing me he had made a list of twenty people who had the most impact on his life and who made him feel loved. I was on that list!

I knew this man for a very brief time and he had done only one Sand Play session with me. I was certain John had connected with the best in himself during his process. Although he did not initially realize it, the Sand Play scene he created re-awakened his desire to write. It has been my experience in the interplay between my soul and the souls of others that it's all in the timing. A few months after he sent that letter he died. His journey in the sand tray is in the "Stories" section titled "The Plan and Approach Has Just Changed."

The stories in this book have the same effect on me today as they did when they first happened. Each sand tray creation is revealing, and when spoken through the *knowing place* of the Soul what comes forth is often profound. The smallest recognitions can transform a life in deep and meaningful ways.

****

As a result of the powerful effect Sand Play had in my sessions with Sung, BJ, Jason and others during those early days of private practice, I founded Sandplay Explorations®: Discovery through Therapeutic Play; a private practice specifically designed for individual counseling sessions and group workshops with adults, couples, children and families. A few years later, I created SandWorks®: Powerful Tools for Creative Solutions, in which I used Sand Play and a variety of other experiential tools for personal growth and awareness; self-discovery; creative problem solving; conflict resolution; mediation; team building; success training; life empowerment and the list goes on. To learn more information on SandWorks® or Sandplay Explorations®, feel free to visit my website: **www.SandWorks.net** or **www.SandPlayfortheSoul.com.**

Barbara Needs a Vacation

One woman, an accomplished editor, publisher, speaker and writer, visited my studio shortly after I founded Sandplay Explorations®. She was curious about my work and how it might assist her. She told me, "I'm in a mentally and emotionally stuck place, and I feel as if my body is falling apart. I'm unhappy in my relationships, exhausted, and my business is stagnant. I just want to free myself and my business from this rut."

I invited her to come and do a sand tray. In less than ninety minutes this accomplished woman discovered a quick and easy solution to her problem right there before her eyes in the scene she created. An item which symbolically represented "the weight of the world" to Barbara was sitting in the middle of a path blocking all her success and hope. I asked her, "What do you need to reach your highest goal?" She viewed her scene and allowed it to speak with just a little facilitating on my part, "I need a vacation," she said as she sighed. "I can't achieve anything if I don't take time out. I'm too exhausted to try for any dream—incredible or not."

I encouraged Barbara to go on the vacation though she claimed there were no resources. Nonetheless the "deserved" vacation took hold in her being, and monies manifested to support this very real need. Her soul spoke loud and clear and she could not refute what was said. When she allowed her *knowing place* to lead the way, the resolve and intent to have it happen proved successful. Barbara went on her vacation to the Yucatan in Mexico for twelve days. Upon her return, a whole new person showed up on my door step with a huge smile. She said, "Paula it's all so simple and clear. I know exactly what I need to do." After that she transformed her business to a whole new level of success. However, she forgot to incorporate into her life one very important piece of information that had shown up in her Sand Play.

Six months after the vacation in the Yucatan, Barbara began working twelve hours plus per day, seven days a week. . .and continued to do so for the next few years. . .trying to keep up with the successful expansion of her publishing company; a success which had come about as a result of the clarity she received during that vacation in the Yucatan.

A few years later an opportunity arose for Barbara to do another session in my studio. This time she sensed something deep inside wanting to speak with her. As I facilitated her through her second journey, her soul spoke once again loud and clear, this time through different means. Barbara could barely talk after creating her scene. She was in ecstasy and told me she was experiencing a feeling as if she was home with her Maker. When Barbara viewed the world she created she felt it was like being in the presence of the "One" who originally caused her to come into physical form.

Barbara traveled to a place so deep within her that the message she was receiving could not be denied. And that is what it took. I have known Barbara for years; she can be a very stubborn lady when it comes to addressing her needs in a healthy manner. Every cell in her body shouted out, "Barbara, take time to experience the divine through 'sacred timeouts.' You are in danger of losing yourself again in your work, especially if you continue to work long hours."

Unfortunately for Barbara, although she did take 'sacred time-outs' and restful vacations more often, it was not enough. In between these brief sabbaticals she continued to work long hours much too often. As a result she made other unhealthy choices, in large part because she was so exhausted and wasn't thinking clearly. Her health deteriorated. She had to sell her business and sold it to a person who was unable to fulfill the contractual agreements. Critical illness and financial ruin went hand in hand. Barbara almost died three times; however, she survived and managed to recreate herself. She remembered the messages her soul revealed to in her sand tray. Barbara finally responded fully to her soul's knowing.

Today she is a healthy and vibrant woman, who is happy with her present career developing and administering an innovative and hugely successful educational program. Gone are the days of working long hours, seven days a week. At the top of Barbara's priority list of self care are traveling, having fun and reading. The sand tray scenes she had previously created remain a reminder to keep her life in balance physically, emotionally, mentally and spiritually.

How Can Miniatures Placed in a Sand Tray Tell the Truth so Clearly and Concisely?

Nearly every person who has done a Sand Play session has felt his or her creation was true to life, revealing far more information than the person thought was possible to receive. Huge obstacles melted away as the information brought forth through the scenes helped clear debris from past traumas; misguided perceptions and assumptions; confused thinking and convoluted emotions. . .all of which had previously blocked them from receiving the information they needed to become unstuck.

Releasing set beliefs and habitual patterns which often hold us captive and causes mental, emotional and physical suffering, is no easy feat. Witnessing those energies as reflected back to us in our tray scenes sheds light and offers a whole new perspective on our current life challenges. A common response clients often have when they view their life scenarios symbolically in their sand trays through the view of their soul is, "This is not as bad as it seems. Dealing with this challenge is doable."

Practitioners working in the fields of mental, physical and spiritual health would be the first to acknowledge that matters of mind, body and emotions can be complex, fueling many challenges in daily living. I do not, nor would I ever claim that Sand Play is "The Answer" to cure or heal what ails us. I do, however, believe that our souls have answers if we will but listen to them. Every person I have facilitated in the sand tray, has a *knowing place* within him or herself that is capable of answering any question needing to be answered and solving any problem needing to be resolved. . .even in the most challenging and seemingly hopeless situations. There are numerous examples of this in the Sand Play Stories section. Each person, if given the opportunity, and acting on that opportunity, can experience this place of knowing. Inspired hope and solutions to life's difficult problems can surface in the most surprising ways.

Can Anyone Do Sand Play?

The answer is "Yes" almost anyone can do it. If you are able to place items in a sand tray, or have someone do it for you, you can participate. All the background information needed to participate in your own Sand Play journey, or a modified variation thereof, is covered in the last section of this book: "How to do Sand Play for the Soul."

The Many Faces of Sand Play

- Part 11 -

"No man can reveal to you aught but that which already lies half asleep in the dawning of your knowledge.

The teacher who walks in the shadow of the temple, among his followers, gives not of his wisdom but rather of his faith and his lovingness.

If he is indeed wise he does not bid you enter the house of his wisdom but rather leads you to the threshold of your own mind.

For the vision of one man lends not its wings to another man.

And even as each one of you stands alone in God's knowledge, so must each one of you be alone in his knowledge of God and his understanding of the earth."

The Prophet
- Kahlil Gibran -

The Soul works in mysterious, transforming ways, especially when it speaks in the sand tray. Only you truly know, even if you do not yet know, the power of your own knowingness yet to be revealed from within. I am but a facilitator to help you awaken the sleeping prophet within.

- Paula Petrovic, the Sand Play Lady -

Sand Play and You

So how does a person begin to understand this unfamiliar and unique way of giving voice to his or her soul? It is crucial that you be open and willing to receive what your soul wishes to say through your Sand Play creations. Before we talk logistics it's valuable to note that being willing to participate in this type of journey requires you to be open to another way of communication with the Self. . .the higher, more expanded version of you. It means you are willing to give yourself a chance to be more than you thought you could be. And all that is required is simply accepting the possibility there may be more to you than meets the eye.

An adventure of this nature only asks that you show up and be present. The Soul will lead the way. The actual journey itself, and what unfolds, offers an opportunity to meet the expanded version of you: The "best in YOU" capable of showing you who you are in the greater scheme of your life. Allowing yourself to receive what your *knowing place* has to offer is the action required to take the next step. Each experience is unique based on the individual's present state of being. How you show up during the process is as valuable as what actually happens during the session. The sand tray and items you place in the tray are the tools to assist you on the journey. The scene you create is a means of communication in which your soul can speak. First and foremost, however, is you, being present, willing and able to participate and receive the messages from the *knowing place* within.

Sand Play and the Soul

More often than not when people hear the words "Sand Play," and do not know of my work, they commonly have one of two types of initial responses. The first is, "What is Sand Play? It sounds like mindless fun!" The second is, "This sounds silly. How can I take something like this seriously?" For the skeptics and curious alike, those daring to do a Sand Play Adventure, are very surprised by what unfolds during the session.

Sand Play and the Business World

In the mid-nineties I participated in training conferences focused on introducing spiritual principles into the business world. While I had an opportunity to learn a lot about the many hidden facets of business, what intrigued me most was the impact my mini sand tray scene had on a number of people at the conference, and what unfolded as a result.

The most common responses were "How cute," "What a novelty," "Looks like fun," then people went on their way to other interests. Those who allowed the time to hear more about Sand Play work were instantly captivated. Though it took effort to gather test subjects, I stuck with my resolve to spread the word about Sand Play to as many people at the conference as were willing to listen. I knew executives, supervisors and managers in the business world could greatly benefit from information received through their sand tray creations. I was steadfast and determined to prove this to be so.

Tom Justin, facilitator, trainer and speaker with Fortune 500 companies, and a presenter at the conferences, was amazed when he entered the world of Sand Play. He wrote:

"My world consists of working with people and corporations who desire personal and financial growth. Through seminars and consultations we work towards those ends, which is not always an easy or successful process.

"I have worked with numerous methods and techniques and reviewed dozens, perhaps hundreds more, from a variety of disciplines. When I first heard about your sand play, I chuckled. I passed it off as a novelty. You were kind enough (and smart enough) to offer me an opportunity to explore this technique. I am very happy that I took you up on it.

"This is one of the quickest and most effective methods I have ever seen in which to bring a person to realization of how they live their life. I continue to chuckle after my experience, but in wonder, that such a seemingly simple concept could have such depth. ...I am most impressed and I hope I can be of help to you in spreading this beyond its current box."

Jack Canfield, co-author of the *Chicken Soup for the Soul* series, who spoke at one of the conferences to an audience of six hundred, walked down from the podium to look closely at my mini-sand tray sitting on the table in front of me. He said, "Now this is an interesting way to get people's attention. It makes me curious about your sand box and what's in it." The sand box has appealed to countless many with its luring embrace.

At the same conference I met Lawrence Lanoff, a delightful person, who at the time was a film producer/director from Los Angeles. It was a pleasure to facilitate two Sand Play sessions with him. He wrote:

> "Thank you for the tremendous body of knowledge and expertise I received with the sand tray work. . . .The work I've done with you is really incredible. My house got completely changed around as a result of the information I received during our session together. I cleaned up my space and my office after realizing from the sand tray that "CLUTTER" had a stronghold on my life.
>
> "Measurable, tangible differences have come about as a result of working with you and the sand trays. I think all people in the creative arts would benefit from explorations in the sand tray."

Successful business man, Jonathan Greenberg, said after his first sand play session:

> ". . .When I first heard about your work I was very skeptical. I didn't understand how it would yield the results I was looking for, yet something told me I should do it—to

take that leap of faith we all do every once in a while. It was one of the smarter decisions I have made.

". . .I've tried many different modalities and read numerous books on how to get past the head games we play on ourselves into the deeper root of our issues. Of all the processes I have done, your sand play work was by far the most efficient and quickest at by-passing the superficial issues and unearthing the real issues I needed to deal with. The benefits from our sessions were numerous and very telling.

"Paula, you have a tremendous tool at your disposal and I can't think of anyone who wouldn't benefit from this process if they very serious about helping themselves. You can rest assured; I'll be back for more sessions."

Jonathan did come back for more sessions. I first worked with him in Los Angeles at the conference where Tom Justin and Jack Canfield were giving their talks. The second time he flew to Sedona from Los Angeles for a weekend intensive. The third time I facilitated a session with him in Malibu Lake, California. Each time he was utterly surprised and transformed by the discoveries he made. The information he received helped affirm and support what needed to be done to successfully promote a unique and informative travel book on a mass scale.

One of the most delightful success stories in the sand tray is the inception and creation of Barry Spilchuk's bestseller *A Cup of Chicken Soup for the Soul*, co-authored with Jack Canfield and Victor Mark Hanson. His book was yet to be written when I first met him. The book caught Barry by surprise when it found its way into his sand tray creation.

In his first Sand Play session the idea for this book surfaced full force. The *knowing place* within, told him it was indeed time to a write a half pint version of *Chicken Soup for the Soul*. The second time I worked with Barry he was gathering stories for his book and under great deal of stress. He came close to giving up on the project because of a huge mental block. Within one hour of creating his scene Barry cleared the block, enabling him to complete his book with greater ease. In gratitude he acknowledged the work we did together in the sand.

Barry, a facilitator, consultant, trainer and speaker to Fortune 500 companies, is a loving soul with a kind heart and the natural ability to make people laugh. He loves introducing the art of joy into the business world. As way of nudging my Sand Play work out of hiding and into the limelight, he wrote the following testimonial and read it to six hundred people at a talk he gave.

"Just a quick note to tell you how "Blown Away" I was as a result of our Sand Tray session! It was such a deep experience that has given me a new sense of FOCUS and has enabled me to clear away a huge mental block that has been causing me much stress. I also have been able to re-establish my priorities so that all the important things in my life are clearly set.

"I am a very open minded person AND I want to be totally honest with you. When I first heard what you wanted us to do (Play in the sand!), the only reason I did it was to honor our professional relationship.

"Personally and professionally, I am so glad we spent the time together. I gained many benefits and I have told numerous colleagues about the amazing Stress Reducing, Healing Benefits of this work. . .I highly recommend Sand Play as a tool to help a person focus and clear up their personal clutter. I am already more productive and enjoying a more balanced lifestyle as a result of my sessions."

In *A Cup of Chicken Soup for the Soul,* Barry credited the Sand Play he did with me in the acknowledgement section of this book stating. "You gave us the tools to love and nurture this project from inception to completion."

Barry's sand tray scene gave him the information he needed to clear his mental blocks and move beyond his stress. This allowed him to actualize his goals; one of which turned out to be a bestseller and has touched the lives of 500,000 plus readers. His soul spoke and he listened.

Sand Play is Full of Delightful Wisdom and Insights

Dialoguing with the Soul is a personal choice and one only you can make.

Thousands of people have dialogued with their souls in the sand tray at my studio, and in other settings. Soon you too will be able to go on a similar journey of your own, in the safety and privacy of your own home, or other personal sacred space. . .if you so choose. The sand tray, collection of miniatures (including personal treasures), the scenes created with selected items, can be easily made available and ready to serve. Whether the creation is done in a traditional sandbox, or on a table, the floor, or wherever the Soul Adventure is guided to take place, the Soul is always ready and willing to share its wisdoms and give guidance—especially if you find yourself in an undesirable predicament and in need of support. All you have to do is ask for help as you might in sacred prayer or in quiet contemplation. The last section of this book covers this more in depth.

If You Meet Buddha in the Sand Tray, Expect a Surprise

Judith came to me with a fear of lack. She was having a difficult time paying her bills—including rent, tuition for her master's degree program, and financially helping a sixteen year-old daughter who had recently given birth to a baby girl. Except for the money issues, she had a positive attitude towards life and was one of the gentlest, sweetest people I have ever known. Her fear of financial lack was a curious phenomenon to her. This fear did not complement her Buddhist beliefs. When she came to see me we set the intent for the energy of money to speak to her through the eyes of Buddha. After she created her scene, I asked her to let this energy speak. She moved easily into a deep meditative state. I asked her to open her eyes, view her tray scene, then I facilitated as she told me about the fear of lack. We experienced chills throughout our bodies as she told her story. It felt as if a magical presence was with us in the room. When Judith tapped into her *knowing place* the message she received about her issues with money were twofold.

The first message had to do with a reality check. Judith recognized that whenever an action required her to spend money, the money was always present to pay what needed to be paid at that moment in time. Her focus on future needs, and expecting the money to be present when the need did not yet exist caused unnecessary complications and stress. The second message had to do with her perception of lack. The question presented was, "What exactly is it you lack? By definition, lack means 'not having.' What is it you need at this moment you do not have?"

Judith tried to answer the question and could not. Instead she realized she was having a wonderful time playing in the sand tray, re-awakening a part of her psyche that understood what the fear of lack was really about. She felt as if Buddha was talking to her directly. "What, exactly, was it she did not have?" Judith and I broke out in laughter. She had come to me to solve a problem that in reality did not exist.

Commentary: After Judith left, I did something I had never done following a session. I basked in the afterglow of the experience that had just taken place. The influence of the energies set in motion during the session, and the far reaching effect it had on her, also profoundly affected me and continued to do so for some time.

I cannot explain why, but after Judith's session I felt a playful, innocent oneness with the world awaken inside me. I sat in the chair and could not leave the studio for another half hour. I was grateful I did not have another client scheduled soon after. I integrated this glorious feeling of light-hearted innocence and sense of oneness, and all felt well in my world. Out of curiosity I asked this feeling dancing inside me, "What or who are you? I'm sure enjoying your presence." It spontaneously responded with a chuckle, "Do I really need to tell you? Who do you think I am?" In that instant I knew. Who else but the

One who helped Judith realize the problem she thought she had in reality did not exist.

Operating with a Full Deck of Cards

When all the facts are in and we know the whole story to the fullest extent possible, making healthy informed choices becomes a natural course of action. Often only a slight shift in attitude is required. When we are operating with a "full deck of cards" and have all the resources available to us, walking through life's trials and tribulations becomes that much easier to handle and digest.

Clients who have had a powerful Sand Play breakthrough session will occasionally ask me, "How is it possible that years of pain and suffering have been suddenly defused and dissipated significantly . . .and even eliminated. . .in only a few simple sessions playing in the sand tray?" I always respond, "When it comes to functioning in the game of life, operating from a full deck of cards involves a very different game than playing from only a partial deck." One journey I facilitated in the sand tray brings home this concept.

Where Did the Fear Go?

One day a lady named Lilly, wife of a client I was working with at the time, came to see me at the request of her husband. Chad, who was dealing with issues of his own resulting from extreme childhood trauma felt constricted and unable to cope with the demands he felt his wife was making on him. He thought the sand tray could help his wife relax her demands enough so he could work through his own overwhelming issues. He was coming out of post traumatic stress syndrome (PTSD) and having flashbacks of horrifying memories. (Chad's journey is covered more in depth in the Sand Play Stories section of the book titled "The Tiger and the Devil.")

Lilly walked into my studio in a state of terror. It was the first time a client had such a reaction. She sat next to the tray and froze.

"I do not know if I can do this," she told me.

I responded, "That's okay, we can just sit here. You do not have to do anything you are not comfortable doing," We sat for a few minutes and chatted about light topics of interest to her.

Lilly relaxed a little and said, "I think I can do this now." I prepared her to move into her *knowing place.*

I began the clearing ritual I do with all my clients by saying to Lilly, "Take a nice deep breath and with each exhale release all events of the day and allow yourself to move into a neutral place to the greatest extent possible." I often vary this clearing by altering the timing and pacing based on the needs of the client. In Lilly's fearful state she needed more time to move cautiously and gradually through this phase. I guided her to take additional deep and relaxing breaths.

The next step was to set the intent. I said, "Allow your *knowing place,* the place that has all the answers, to show what you most need to know about your life at this time." I also walked Lilly through the intent setting phase of the facilitation slowly and carefully. Then I asked Lilly to pick the miniatures she was most drawn to and place them in her sand tray scene. With great intensity Lilly selected her miniatures. It was clear something was deeply troubling her. She created her scene and returned to her former frightened state. I asked her what was scaring her.

"The miniatures in my sand tray. . .I did not want to pick them up but they made me and now I feel afraid."

I asked, "Do all the miniatures you placed in your tray make you feel this way?"

She replied, "Oh no, not every one."

"Can you tell me which ones don't?"

Lilly proceeded to tell which ones she felt good about and why. As I facilitated her through the sand play process, she tuned into the symbolism of each of these figures and how she felt about them. She began to feel less afraid and safer within herself. As she explored the significance of each figure and how they related to her tray scene, she felt empowered and soon relaxed completely. Finally we approached the figures that had frightened her. A huge smile came across her face and she said, "These figures aren't so scary anymore. How is that possible? When I first picked them I was so afraid of how they made me feel; now it's not such a big deal. What happened? Where did the fear go?"

I told her about my "operating from a full deck" theory. When she first came to me she was in a place of fear. When she selected the miniatures, she was still fearful, and could only focus her attention on the figures generating fear because that was the state she was in. In the process of creating her scene she had not paid conscious attention to the rest of the figures she selected. She only saw those figures that caused her to be afraid because her fear was in control. The intent had already been set for her to select miniatures reflecting what she most needed to know about her life at this time. . .and that is what the *knowing place of soul* did. When I helped her to focus on the figures that were not frightening to her she shifted emotional gears and experienced other types of feelings, not only fear. The other miniatures she had selected, and didn't realize at the time, were actually of images which empowered her and gave her self-confidence. When the attention turned to those empowered parts of herself, it put her in a different frame of mind and emotional disposition. A fuller range of emotions and thought processes was with her and she was now able to operate from a "full deck of cards."

When Lilly could address the figures she feared, she could do so from a more informed state of being. It was no longer only fear facing fear; it was also the empowered, more confident Lilly included in the interaction. The empowered Lilly was also present. Her higher functioning self was operational and participating in the exchange.

When fear is dealing with fear, more fear is generated. When wisdom, strength and confidence enter the scene, what happens to fear? It changes form. . .how can it not? Lilly soon recognized what had happened. She realized dealing with fear from a fearful place froze her in a state of terror to a point of non-functioning. When she stepped into a stronger, more empowered, place of being, the game changed. She was no longer at the mercy of her fear. She had other options.

Lilly also had a traumatic childhood. With regard to her marriage she was just as wounded and in need of support and love as her husband. She desperately sought this from a man who, not unlike herself, was dealing with a lot of emotional wounds and pain. At the time, neither could be there for the other until they could help and care for themselves. Relying solely on the other spouse to address and take care of their needs was unrealistic and causing further stress. The last I heard, they were doing much better together as a couple. Each was allowing the other private time to work on their own traumatized childhood issues.

Sand Play in Celebration

One lady came to me to do a birthday tray for herself. She created a scene in celebration of her 60th birthday. . .rich, colorful and reflective of all the wonderful experiences now blessing her life, Susan broke into tears of joy. Over the years she had undergone major obstacles yet was still in one piece, alive and living life to the fullest. To see her soul display its' knowing before her eyes in such a visual display—how much she had accomplished and how well she had done for herself in life—affirmed her success and brought her a deep sense of fulfillment. This radiated throughout the entire room as a result of her experience with the sand tray scene

Sand Play for the Human Service and Health Care Field

Sand Play, as utilized in my private practice, has taken on many roles. Some of my most powerful experiences were when I did contract work for the Verde Valley Sanctuary, a shelter for battered women and children, and Desert Canyon Treatment Center for Drug and Alcohol Rehabilitation.

Anne Cunningham, founder and former administrator for the Verde Valley Sanctuary and current co-owner and Assistant Director of Desert Canyon Treatment Center, describes the essence of the Sand Play work I did for these two organizations.

"Paula Petrovic has been contracted to facilitate therapeutic sand tray play sessions for our clients at Desert Canyon since it first opened in July, 1998. Our facility is an alternate drug and alcohol treatment center for adults. Paula does sessions with our clients, usually in the fourth week of their program. Since she first began with us, Paula has demonstrated extraordinary skill in facilitating our clients to deepen their experiences and understanding of their therapeutic process. Often it is the sand play session that our clients say 'brings all the treatment work together for them.'

"In 1997 and 1998, I also worked with Paula at Verde Valley Sanctuary, a 23-bed domestic violence shelter for women and children. As Executive Director, I saw a great need to have some way to do intensive therapy with clients who were unwilling to share what had happened to them. When I first heard about Paula's work utilizing sand play and other experiential therapies, I asked her to set up and facilitate a sand play program at the shelter.

"Her program was hugely successful and of great benefit to the residents. For example, one Native American family was traumatized witnessing a violent act, and then was threatened with the same type of punishment if they told. Their culture prohibited them from talking about this. 'We can't burden others with our problems,' said the mother. The sand trays of each of the children told of the tragic happening and Paula was able to help the mom and children be open to resolve the issue, and get help and begin to heal.

"Any agency, particularly those dealing with people in distress, would greatly benefit form Paula's work. We are grateful for the wisdom, insight and facilitation of sand tray work for our clients."

Many heart-warming and magical moments took place during my sessions with these clients. They journeyed in the sand tray and the scenes they created quickly and clearly affirmed they were indeed on the right track. Coming to these agencies for help and being able to experience that there is life beyond trauma and hardship was a major step in a healthy direction. These people survive tremendous challenges and ordeals. To be willing and trusting enough to receive assistance requires great courage and commitment on their part. When an individual is able to heal and live their life in healthy, constructive, wholesome manner, those they love—even their neighbors—all greatly benefit.

The "Sacred Seven"

- Part III -

"Spirit works in mysterious ways,
The Sacred Seven are among its three
dimensional messengers."

-As told to Paula Petrovic in metaphor
through the Fontanini Angel-

Through observation, reflection, and asking questions about your creation, the Soul is given a voice to dialogue with you more directly in a tangible form. The information received takes you down paths of delightful discovery and revelation.

- Paula Petrovic, the Sand Play Lady -

Seven Keys to Unlocking the Magic and Mysteries of Sand Play

Before me is the wooden sand tray made by the loving hands of my dear friend Jim. It holds a scene containing the "Sacred Seven". . .a set of figures I was guided to spontaneously place in the sand tray after questioning my *knowing place* regarding the Sand Play book I was to write. I asked, "Where do I begin and what do I say?" Within moments of inquiry and creating my scene, the Sacred Seven were birthed. Soon into the self-facilitation process the figures symbolically came to life, awakening a higher knowing within me that would assist me to write this book over the ensuing months until its completion.

The first words spoken as I dialogued with the Sacred Seven in the sand tray for the first time came as a group message:

"We are a source of encouragement and inspiration . . .your soul's way of reminding you that you will not be alone during the creation of this book. Should you find yourself ever doubting the value or your ability to write it, we will serve to remind you that this creation is indeed worthy of being born and that you are the right person to do the birthing. The only request we make is that you allow yourself to see us visually while working on your book. Whether we remain in your sand tray, or are placed in another location, our presence will help activate the know-ing within, you do not always hear due to self-doubt. Allow us to assist through seen and unseen ways to unlock the magic and mysteries of this creation, and we will be there to guide and support you. Enjoy the journey. "

Receiving this message solidified my commitment: No matter what self-defeating insecurities were lurking in the background and attempting to wreak havoc on my psyche, the project went full speed ahead until its completion. The message from the "Sacred Seven" was most auspicious and taken to heart.

For a long time I had serious reservations about this project, even though several people encouraged me to write about Sand Play. . .the way I do it. It took me years to realize this book had a fate of its own, and that I needed to get out of the way of its destiny, and over my fear of going public and spreading the word. The fact remains, and has, since I first fell in love with Sand Play: The Soul loves dialoguing in three-dimensional form with anyone wishing to venture into new territories of exploration, discovery and realization. . .from the expanded version of who they are in the grand design of their lives.

The "Sacred Seven"

Seven key components need to be present during a *Sand Play for the Soul* experience to receive the most benefit. The messages I received and the wisdoms imparted to me by the Sacred Seven helped me write this book, making the power and magic of Sand Play available to you, my readers. Learning to dialogue with the Soul in three-dimensional form is as simple as playing in the sandbox with a life-transforming twist.

The Seven Key are:
1. Purity and Innocence
2. The Quiet Space
3. The Open and Willing Mind
4. The Wise Mentor
5. The Ancient
6. The Divine
7. The Sand Tray

The Soul and the Sacred Seven

The element of surprise always brings a smile to clients' faces when they create their tray scene and dialogue with their souls. They never know what to expect when they first arrive. By the time they leave they know exactly what is going on inside themselves that caused them problem(s) and made their life difficult and unpleasant. . .and in some cases a living hell! **No problem is too big for the Soul to address.** In the *knowing place* my clients frequently discover, after observation and reflection, that what they thought was going on is not what is really going on. The key is asking the right questions. You too can discover and dialogue with your soul using the Seven Keys, as seen through the eyes of the Sacred Seven. Questions needing to be asked and answers needing to be heard can symbolically come to life and realized in the sand tray.

When you create a sand tray scene everything that unfolds is moment to moment. The empty tray soon becomes filled with wisdom, purpose and clarity via the miniatures you select then place in the tray to create the scene. Through observation, reflection, and asking questions about your creation, the Soul is given a voice to dialogue with you more directly in a tangible form. The information received takes you down paths of delightful discovery and revelation.

When the Soul is involved, expect the unexpected, and know that whatever unfolds, *Sand Play for the Soul* allows you to commune with the expanded version of you: "the best in you" as viewed through the eyes of the Soul. The Sacred Seven provides a vehicle of communication in which to do the journey and Sand Play provides the three-dimensional visual.

Awakening the Sacred Seven

"What treasures are living in your home asking to be found and brought to life?" Your personal "Sacred Seven" may be only moments away from entering your life and awakening in you a knowing so revealing and profound that life as you know it could permanently change for the better. They could be sitting on a shelf, tucked away in a closet or dresser, or in your basement. . .or they may be a person, living or in spirit, who has touched you so deeply that just being in their presence activates the divine qualities of the Sacred Seven. You may be surprised to find that the very keys to unlock the doors of a mystery in your life—hankering to be solved—do exist and are available and within reach. For me the discovery of my Sacred Seven was simple and profound. For you it will be reflected through how you receive the information and stories presented throughout the remainder of this book, and what you do with what you learn as a result.

The Sacred Seven of *Sand Play for the Soul*

My dear friend Terry gave me a photo which represented "Purity and Innocence." My sister gifted me the figurines which brought to life "The Open and Willing Mind" and "The Wise Mentor." "The Quiet Space" came in the form of a figurine once belonging to my grandmother who died when I was two. "The Ancient" and "The Divine" were living on the shelves of my studio as part of my Sand Play collection. And finally the sand tray built by my ex-husband, Jim, completed the Sacred Seven. Upon their birthing, I soon discovered that qualities inherent in the "Sacred Seven," are what allowed *Sand Play for the Soul* to fulfill its highest purpose: To help awaken, guide, support, and actualize "the highest and best you."

The First Key: Purity and Innocence

When I created the tray scene which brought the "Sacred Seven" to my attention, the first item selected for my scene was a dearly treasured framed photo of my godchild Olivia at one-month old, with her little head nestled under her mother's cheek.

To this very day, every time I see this picture my eyes become misty and my heart feels embraced by a deep sense of joy. This moment of a mother/child connection captures purity and innocence in its highest form. When I spontaneously put this photo in my tray scene it became obvious why my soul had me do so.

71

Purity and innocence is one of the driving forces behind the Sand Play work. It makes no claims, or demands of anyone. . . it just is. It happens automatically and only takes a person as far as he or she is willing and able to go. One of the most common re-marks made by clients when I facilitate a Sand Play process is the non-threatening quality of the work.

Purity and innocence is one of the driving forces behind the Sand Play work. It makes no claims, or demands of anyone. . . it just is.

Playing in the sand and creating the scenes feels safe. There is no right or wrong. What unfolds is organic, natural and unconditional in its expression. The only thing the process requires of us is to show up and be present while we create our scenes.

When Olivia and I spend time together, we are so happy to be in each other's presence. I know she and I are connecting with each other at a Soul level. We laugh, play and celebrate our true connection from a place of pure love and innocence. We feel no need to prove or defend who we are in each other's presence. We are just joyfully present for each magical moment of sharing. This is innocence and purity in living form.

The Soul speaking in the sand tray is a similar feeling. The scenes created evoke a sense of purity and innocence, like that of a loving connection with a child. In this instance the child is you.

I believe that each and every person comes into the world innocent and pure. Innocence and purity is our natural state of being when we first arrive into our earthly existence. As newborns our life slate starts clean. Creating a sand tray scene begins from that state of purity and innocence. You start with an empty tray of sand (a clean slate) and begin from there. There is no required outcome. What unfolds is unique to the individual and based on present need. The *knowing place* within is the Soul's base of operation. It expresses what we need to know at any given moment. The sand tray scene provides the three dimensional visual to reflect that knowing. A person's best qualities, talents and abilities are always evident in the scenes created, no matter what the scene looks like. How can it not? We are starting from a fresh clean slate.

How do I know this? I know from the look on their faces, the tone in their voice and what they say. "Is this really me? My tray scene shows me I am so much more than I thought myself to be. I want to feel more of this experience in my life. I would have never believed I was so capable and aware had I not seen it with my own eyes." Even during the most challenging moments of initial discovery. . .when getting to the truth sometimes requires going through a detour created by deceiving lies or a harmful past. . .even then the Soul always creates a spark of knowing and hope in the individual that all is not lost. Even clients who have experienced extreme hardship and trauma in their lives walk out the door smiling. No matter what my clients have been through in life, when they accept an opportunity to access their soul's knowing, a breakthrough occurs. When we allow the state of purity and innocence to enter our consciousness, starting over from a clean slate makes recreating our lives so much easier and attainable.

Are there treasures in your home, or people in your life, that evoke a sense of purity and innocence within you—perhaps gifts given to you (handmade or bought), photos of loved ones—especially children, works of art that touch your heart, a child's toy, a pet. . .the list goes on? For me, it's the photo of Olivia and her mom. These meaningful representations of our three dimensional world have the potential to open doors to untapped regions of our psyche yearning to be given a voice. Purity and innocence are necessary components when dialoguing with the Soul in the sand tray, or an alternate sacred holding space.

The Second Key: The Open and Willing Mind

The next of the Sacred Seven to reveal itself in the tray scene was a ceramic figure of an Asian baby sitting on a stack of books, wearing spectacles and smiling while reading. The figurine reflects the image of one who is wide open and willing to fully experience the world in which he lives. This child is curious, receptive and eager to experience his entire environment.

Babies are not discerning in what they learn. From the moment they enter the world their minds and senses are wide open. They receive immense amounts of information at an astounding rate. Learning basics as complex as crawling, sitting up, walking, and talking are all essential to one day survive and function on their own. In those pre-toddler years of life we do not think about all we need to accomplish. We do not stew over whether we are good enough, or able to succeed. The learning just happens as a natural and automatic process.

When you spontaneously surrender to the process of creating your tray scene and allow it to reveal its story, you have begun dialoguing with your soul. If the mind is open and willing to experience what occurs during this natural and organic process, the channels of communication with your *knowing place* begin to awaken your senses and awareness.

What possible representations in your life environment awaken the qualities of an open and willing mind within you? The figurine of the baby reading on a stack of books sits in my bedroom next to my computer. Every day he reminds and awakens within me the qualities of an open and willing state of mind. I am not surprised he is part of the Sacred Seven group. One of the most crucial components to doing Sand Play is the openness and willingness to do the process. Without those qualities dialoguing with the Soul in the sand tray cannot take place.

The Third Key: The Quiet Space

Perched on his gold rock, connected to the earth, solid and grounded, sits a Buddha miniature, the third of the Sacred Seven to enter in my sand tray. He is clear, present and open to all possibilities from his quiet center within as he communes with the earth's elements and the others in the sand tray. His energy awakens within me the knowing that there is no hasty action, or need to do "something" to feel purpose and meaning in my life. Everything is as it should be. Whatever needs to take place will happen when the timing is right. He also makes a point of reminding me that premature action can lead to much stress, confusion and chaos. The results may be the opposite of what was intended.

It is risky business trying to be in control from a place of neediness. Every time I lust after a particular outcome, something different happens, and it's rarely welcomed. If I do not force the outcome to be a certain way, and allow my soul to lead, whatever unfolds always ends up better than I ever anticipated.

I couldn't do the Sand Play work if I did not operate from a neutral space with clients. The Buddha meditating on his gold rock tells me;

> "Go to the quiet space and allow yourself to be guided from a place of quiet surrender and innocence. Only when the connection is made in this quiet surrender and innocence are you set to begin the journey. Only then will you be guided to make choices and take actions that awaken and stir those parts of you seeking your attention. Through the symbolism, and embracing qualities of the choices made and actions taken, your soul will speak. Before you can begin the process, however, you must have a quiet space within you to hear the voice of your soul and what it has to offer."

When the mind is too busy with thoughts, there is no room for the *knowing place* to speak. Taking deep, relaxing breaths, releasing all the events of the day, and allowing yourself to move into a neutral space, sets the intent for entering the place of knowing.

Whenever I take time out from my thoughts and center myself in the quiet space, I find I am able to breathe and just be. . .without the urgency of feeling I must do it right now or else! Being a multi-task-oriented person by nature, taking time out is crucial to stay in balance. When my glass is full, there is no room for more. If what is contained in the glass is stale, there is no room to be replenished with something fresh and rejuvenating. It is essential to keep the human vessel as clear as possible, in order to be available to receive Divine abundance.

Who or what helps you move into place of quiet surrender and allows you space to receive the abundant offerings and knowing of the Soul?

The Fourth Key: The Wise Mentor

Next is the figure who calls himself the Wise Mentor. He is perched on a mound of sand in the center of my sand tray scene ready to share what he knows to be true about Sand Play. (Whenever, I feel doubt gathering strength and saying, "I'm in way over my head with this book and can not possibly do this," I am reminded that Truth is a priceless commodity.)

As I look upon this figure with long white hair and brown robe, holding his staff, I am guided to take a deep, relaxing breath. As I do so I feel a calm and unassuming presence comes over me and I know Truth is speaking to me through my Wise Mentor. I hear his voice in the distant reaches of my mind saying:

> "Let us review the facts, dear one. In all the years you have done this work has any information received by a person from their Sand Play creations ever been questionable in merit and integrity? Focus on the essence of the work itself. . .what it truly is and offers people who are willing and wanting to experience more depth and substance in their lives. Since it is you who have been present during their creation process, you know the stories and the powerful effect of their journeys taken. . .who but you to tell the tales of their amazing discoveries and breakthroughs. "

I am reminded again of why I am writing this book.

On many occasions I found it easy to find excuses to not write. Going public with my work was very scary. As my mind rambled and I questioned my ability, I heard my Mentor's voice, gently nudging me to listen:

> "Remember, dear one, this is not about you; it is about the work flowing through you. If you step aside and let the work lead the way, the same flow will occur in all that you do whenever needed. The work speaks for itself and you are the conduit. Relax and enjoy the journey. This is not about you. It is time to get out of your own way."

It can be daunting to realize I am a mere speck in the greater whole when it involves the vastness of the soul's knowing. However, when it comes to dialoguing with this knowing, I am blessed to have witnessed innumerable, life-altering breakthroughs and revelations in the sand tray. I have never experienced anything else like it. . .and the really exciting part is that this immense "knowing" is there for anyone to tap into, and little is required of us to do so.

Whenever questions became too big and overwhelming to answer on my own, I call in a support system of unquestionable integrity. I turn to my soul and the sand tray to bring clarity, awareness and insight during my most trying life-challenges.

I remember a few years back when business was slow. I felt certain it was time to close down the studio. It broke my heart because I did not want to give up doing Sand Play. Just as I was about to close my business, I created a scene in my sand tray to be sure I was making the right choice. After I had completed it, I heard a knowing voice from deep within me, being very clear and to the point:

> "Ah, excuse me. Are you forgetting something? Aren't you the one who recently assisted a desperate husband to realize he really did not want to kill his wife? You helped him to understand it was the anger and frustration running amuck inside of him that wanted to do this deadly deed. When he saw what was really on going on through his sand tray scene, his whole perspective changed immediately. He was reminded he has two wonderful and amazing children. So the question I pose, in case I'm missing something. . .are you sure it's really time to close down the studio?"

A few days after this self-tray session, my attitude and my business changed. New clients arrived, in part because this man—who decided that killing his wife was not a wise course of action—referred a number people to me. Everyone, even the facilitator, needs some wise assistance now and then. My Wise Mentor is the "Voice of Truth" and is there for me whenever I forget and need to be reminded of the truth.

After working with this metaphor for weeks, he is firmly planted in my conscious mind whether he's physically present or not. You too can find a Wise Mentor symbol that awakens the knowing part of you that serves as a "Voice of Truth" while under its' tutelage. Perhaps you know someone living, or in spirit, who serves this role, or maybe there is a sacred item in your home that evokes a wise and truthful knowingness within.

Wouldn't it be a glorious and intriguing possibility if you were to have a Wise Mentor present at your beck and call? Imagine every time a negative and self-defeating thought occurs, you receive this gentle nudge in the back of your thought process setting the record straight:

"You are worthy, deserving and able to accomplish your goals. You can reach the greatest heights of success possible when the 'best in you' is allowed to be expressed. Ask and you shall receive all the help and knowing you need to achieve what you most desire and yearn to create in your life!"

The Fifth Key: The Ancient

In the summer of 1986, Tibet experienced a brief and temporary reprieve from the Chinese occupation of their country. Tourists and backpackers like me were allowed relative freedom to explore certain parts of this ancient land. Soon after, all that changed and the Tibetan people's story turned a sad page. I was blessed with the opportunity to taste the purity, magnificence and depth of this magical land and its people during a lull in those tumultuous times. These gentle yet cautious people wanted the world to know what was happening in their country.

Tibetan culture has spiritual roots going back to an ancient know-ing and wisdom which seems as if it originates from the beginning of Time itself. While in the presence of the great Himalayas, their monasteries, and chanting monks, I felt connected and alive. In the weeks I spent in Tibet traveling over land from Lhasa to Katmandu, I was in an altered state of consciousness most of the time. Though the high altitude certainly contributed to this euphoric feeling, I knew it was much more than that.

One of my first clients, Sung (the eight year old Tibetan boy I spoke of earlier), touched me so deeply with his innocence and "other worldly" stories in the sand tray. Our exchanges, along with the positive results he experienced are one of the main reasons I pursued Sand Play more seriously.

The more he played in the tray and told me what was transpiring in his created worlds, the more connected and at peace he was.

Sung created scenes containing stories from multiple realities and time frames. The more he played in the tray and told me what was transpiring in his created worlds, the more connected and at peace he was with something not even I fully understood. It appeared there were no limitations to where his mind could travel. It was almost as if time stood still—past, present and future merged as one. All that truly existed was the moment, and in that moment everything and anything was possible.

The Ancient is the fifth of "Sacred Seven" helping to support and guide me during the writing of this book. When I tune into the symbolic image of this figure standing in my sand tray, Tibet, and all that happened during my travels there, these words surface, "Much is yet to be revealed." Sand Play and the tray scenes created are universal and in their varying script there is much hidden in stories yet to be revealed. Their themes touch upon many histories existing throughout time.

The Ancient in my tray scene asks me to remember Sung's expressions and my 1986 summer trek in Tibet—how I felt, who I met, what I did. I am told these experiences are interconnected with who I am today and the Sand Play work I do. He also asks me to be present and attentive in the Now and reminds me that time exists only in the human constructs of reality. The majority of cultures and societies on this planet, especially in the Western Hemisphere, rely on time. When doing a sand tray, time tends to stands still and all that exists are you, the sand tray, your collected miniatures, creating a scene, and the *knowing place.*

Do you remember the last time you were doing something creative—building something for your home, doing a craft project, drawing, writing, planting bulbs in a garden. . .an activity that allowed you to express yourself in some creative manner, and in doing so you became so focused you lost track of time? It's as if time did not exist, only you and the activity you were doing held your full attention. The Sand Play journey is similar.

When you tune out the outer world—people and daily reality— and all that exists is the exchange between you, your soul, and sand tray scene, something magical happens that defies logic. It is a "Now" moment, where one is fully present, in a place of well-being. All the fears and worries from your past, present or future seem to disappear. In this place, another realm of awareness and clarity becomes available and answers to questions long sought simply appear.

What impresses clients the most during a Sand Play session is the ease with which they enter such an empowered place of self-knowing and how uplifting and good it feels. They often say, "I never realized that was going on. . .can it be that simple to resolve?"

Whom do you know, or what among your personal treasures, might be able to help awaken the wisdom and knowing of the Ancient within? Maybe there is someone inside or outside your home environment; or even in the spiritual realm; or your memory banks; or a sacred object of deep significance that may inspire and activate the energy of the Ancient.

Clarity and awareness offers answers to long sought questions seeking to be resolved. Being in the Now allows you to connect with "a knowing" so present and available that fears and worries intruding in your life vanish. I invite you to look for a symbol that could ignite the power of the Ancient.

The Sixth Key: The Divine

The Fontanini Angel, the sixth member of my "Sacred Seven" team, introduced herself in the sand tray, arms spread open in offering grace saying:

> "I am here to remind you of the sacredness of the work and what it offers. You are blessed to walk this sacred Soul journey with others through their world creations, and now it's time to take another step: to take the work to a larger audience. . .sharing this sacred process with those who might not otherwise have the opportunity to participate in such a journey."

I understand what my Angel is saying. I do not need to be present for the Sand Play adventure to begin. You take some basic, simple actions and that's it. In truth, the tools for the work can come in many shapes and forms. Although the sand tray and miniatures are fun and engaging tools to work with, they are not an absolute necessity. When dialogue is in full bloom between you and your knowing soul, magic happens. Inspiration, guidance and support appear, however, a sand tray filled with miniatures is not the only means of tapping into your *knowing place*. Sand Play is certainly a unique, powerful and pleasurable experience; however, there are many pathways to the Soul. You can learn more about other options in the section on "Alternative Approaches to Sand Play."

Your *knowing place* is with you wherever you go. In the last section of this book I offer tips on how to open up and allow yourself to dialogue with your soul, even when you feel it's not in your means to do so. The truth is your soul needs no one but you to ask for its guidance. My book and me are merely an aide and resource base to assist in the dialogue process.

Sand Play, true to its intent, as referred to in this book, is a highly engaging tool to help open doors of communications between you and your soul; however, my Fontanini Angel also informs me:

"Spirit works in mysterious ways and the Sacred Seven are among its highly revered three—dimensional messengers."

She reminds me that:

"Communing in the place of the divine is magnificent and glorious. Just remember, time is often necessary to integrate the results of this sacred union into everyday life. The information and wisdom gained through communing with the Divine will find its way into all that you do. Do not fear, the work itself will work with you and through you, to help this happen.

"Remember the work is about much more than the materials and process used. These are tools to work with during the process but they are not the work itself. . .this you know. There are many creative ways to accommodate and modify any transformational process in order to meet a persons needs. What is most crucial is a willingness to allow the connection with the Soul to come into being, and creating avenues of possibility in which it can be expressed and nurtured.. I am the spiritual voice within you allowing you to hear and be embraced by The Divine. Whenever you are feeling lost, alone or seeking guidance 'ask and ye shall receive' and I will be there to support you always."

My Angel knows what I do not always see. Sometimes I am out of sorts and not in best form. When this happens, I call in The Divine for extra assistance, above and beyond what is normally necessary. Often I go into my studio, or another sacred space, to do a personal clearing. Then I set an intent to be totally clear, present and available from my *knowing place*, and then I do a sand tray scene, or another personal ritual, to help reconnect with what I often refer to as "the magic of life." Soon I am back in my center and ready to engage "the best in me" with the daily world in partnership with my soul's knowingness. Within a short time I feel more connected and confident that all is well, as was intended to be.

Sand Play is immensely helpful in times of challenging upsets, to bring unconscious thoughts, desires and needs to the forefront when they need to be addressed. Its visual and tangible form makes it real and accessible to the conscious mind. The saying "A picture paints a thousand words" is true. I will add, "The sand tray scene paints ten thousand more."

When a person arrives to do a Sand Play Adventure we clear the mind of busy thoughts and set the intent for the session. That is when Divine magic happens and our souls connect. The person creates his or her sand tray scene, communes with their creation through their soul, and the experience deepens. The Divine is fully at work behind the scenes.

During this phase of the Sand Play experience, participants feel present, in the moment, and they feel great! Sometimes the initial connection with the "oneness" or "now" state happens gradually whereas other times it occurs almost immediately. Often the connection between the individual and his or her soul is felt so deeply, and the resulting discoveries the person makes can be so profound, tears are shed. Something wonderful and transforming happens and crying becomes a natural release. (I keep a box of tissues underneath the tray for those magical moments.)

It can be an immense and empowering experience for the individual to be in this state of sacred connection. It is not a place many of us can remain on a regular basis. If we were more able to stay in such a state, the world would be a more loving and welcoming place to live.

There are times I find myself especially drawn to a particular piece, or cluster of pieces, from my studio or personal treasures, which help me enter this space of sacred connection. I will put the item(s) somewhere in my house where I can see them easily or in my sand tray. When I do, it helps me deal with challenging emotional and mental upsets in a more healthy and effective manner. The Fontanini Angel, in particular, often ends up in one of my sacred arrangements. With her arms and hands in an opening embrace, she encourages me to remain open and receptive to The Divine. She reminds me, "I am not alone. There is more to be seen and heard. Allow this knowing in."

Are there special objects of spiritual or religious significance in your home that may want to make themselves known and heard through sacred exchange and facilitation? Perhaps they would like to express themselves to you in the sand tray, or on a shelf, or surface of a special piece of furniture? Images, thoughts and impressions are alive in you and ready to be revealed from the knowingness of your soul. If you are open and willing to explore this possibility, you may be very surprised what unfolds and is revealed.

The Final of the Sacred Seven—the Seventh Key: The Sand Tray

The Sacred Ones have spoken through the creation of my scene in the sand tray. In this sacred space, mystery, intrigue, revelation and resolution have also found their way into thousands of lives. . .and continue to do so. The mini-tray I carried with me when traveling with my work also touches many people's lives. (This beautiful wooden box crafted by a master woodworker is the smaller version of the original tray.) The size, style and construction of my sand trays are what my soul wanted me to have. Your soul may guide you to create a different type of tray or sacred holding space. . .a personal altar perhaps . . .in which to give three dimensional form to the *knowing place* of the Soul.

Since the *knowing place* is vast. . .without boundaries or restrictions. . .the sand tray, and scenes created within its walls, allows our consciousness to view the information received in a structured and digestible form our minds can comprehend. This grounding quality gives us the ability to translate and integrate what is received into tangible form easily accessible for us to use in our daily lives. Most teachers of Sand Play Therapy suggest that the sand tray should be no larger than the peripheral vision available to our viewing eyes. This makes the scene easier to process by its maker. Although I agree with this suggestion, I feel that ultimately only you know what will work best for you.

How I do Sand Play may not be how you decide to craft your unique journeys and dialogues with the *knowing place* of your soul. I simply present an opportunity, some tools and a few guidelines to help you initiate initial contact. . .you fill in the details. In the final representation of the "Sacred Seven," the sand tray tells me, "Just think how many more people will now be able to embark on an amazing Soul Adventure in this simple box filled with sand."

Conclusion of Passage with the "Sacred Seven"

I have opened myself to the wisdom of my "Sacred Seven" and listened to their guidance. They are as much a part of me and Life as I am of them. . .they are extensions of myself. Whenever I am feeling disconnected to the magic and sacredness of life, I turn to them as I would a friend and ask for their support. As my inferior attitude is transmuted into something wholesome and life-affirming, we once again unite.

If you follow the basic principles of the Sacred Seven and allow your soul to lead the way, who knows what can unfold? This format offers a basic foundation from which to begin exploring and dialoguing with your Soul. As you open up more readily to the *knowing place,* receiving continual benefits becomes like breathing air – a completely natural process. Once the choice is made to enter this realm of heightened clarity and awareness and the channels of communication open, you become the master creator. . .the way is yours to lead.

Sand Play Stories

- Part IV -

You can learn more about a person in an
hour of play than in one year
of conversation.

-Plato-

*The stories in this section are true accounts of Sand Play sessions I have facilitated in my studio or while traveling with my work. The names of the people who have experienced these *Sand Play for the Soul Adventures*, and places they live, were changed to protect their privacy except in the first story. Len suggested I use his name.

Through the eyes of the soul,
Radiates gentle wisdom,
In the words that teach,
And a heart that loves,
Shines a presence,
A knowingness in purest form.

- Paula Petrovic, the Sand Play Lady -

Physician Heal Thyself

Len was a physician "extraordinaire" and surgeon in his early fifties. His passion for preventive medicine and alternative healing modalities fed his soul. He studied, worked, and traveled round the world, going where he was guided to master his craft in the art of healing. At one point in his career he worked at Dr. Andrew Weil's world renowned clinic in Tucson, Arizona. He also trained with the Dalai Lama's doctors in northern India and was a mission doctor on Easter Island. He had a stellar resume, and this man would travel fifty miles on a house visit to help a patient. It seemed there would be no stopping him—until fate intervened. The good doctor was diagnosed with a brain tumor and wasn't expected to live. Knowing as much as he did about medicine and alternative healing, he decided this diagnosis was not going to ruin his life. He realized that he needed to take time off to reassess his situation and figure out what on earth was going on with his body.

During my first year in private practice, I met Len at a social gathering in Sedona. He asked what I did and I told him of my Sand Play work. Len was fascinated and wanted to come in for a session. He felt his brain tumor had something it wanted to say to him, and I fully agreed. For a man of this stature and brilliance, with his skills and talents, something was definitely amiss. During his remarkable and busy life, the cancer had awakened with full force to wreak havoc in his physical body. It was trying to get his attention and had succeeded.

Len walked into my studio with a huge smile, his head almost touching the ceiling. He hugged me as soon as he walked through the door and it felt like a giant teddy bear was embracing me with love from the top of my head to the bottom of my feet. After we briefly chatted, we did a visualization to clear the mind and set the intent for the session. Then he set off to create his sand tray scene with great enthusiasm. . .gathering miniatures from the shelves he was most drawn to and placing them in his scene. By the time he finished it was jam packed with items that reflected how he viewed his current world. The scene was rich in color, detail oriented, and VERY BUSY.

Paula: Len, where are you in the tray scene?

Len: I'm not in the tray.

Paula: Why?

Len: Because there is no place for me to be in my world.

Paula: What does that say to you?

Len: My world is so busy there's no time or space for me.

Paula: How does that feel?

Len: Exhausting.

Paula: Where does your tumor fit in the scene?

Len: It's showing me what I'm doing to myself.

Paula: What specifically is it showing you?

Len: My life has become so busy, I'm over-extended and my body has rebelled. There is no place in my life for just me. No time to rest, relax or have play time for myself. I don't exist as a person, only as a doctor. Don't get me wrong, I love helping people heal but in this world I created, and see before me in the sand tray, I literally have no space left for me to be a regular person with needs and wants.

Paula: Is this what your tumor wants you to know?

Len: I'd say it's speaking loud and clear! I'm killing myself by working way too much. Even now I'm busy helping my friends with their health problems, and I should be resting.

Paula: Is there anyone in your tray that can resolve this dilemma?

Len: No.

Immediately following this comment Len was instantly drawn to something on the other side of the room. He spontaneously grabbed a giant plush animal known as "Watch Puppy", a favorite of my younger clientele, and hugged him tight.

Paula: What does "Watch Puppy" have to say about what's happening in your life at this time?

Len: I need to do loving things for myself. How I'm living my life is not in a loving way. I'm killing myself, squelching myself out of existence. No wonder my body is rebelling. It's taking a malignant tumor in my brain to get my attention. Well, it's time to change my ways . . .or else. It's time for "the physician to heal thyself" or my stay on earth will be over shortly.

As I brought the session to a close I asked him how it felt to be holding "Watch Puppy" and hearing what he had just said.

Len smiled, "It feels playful to be holding a giant stuffed animal, and freeing to hear myself say it's my turn to receive loving attention, and to make space in my life for me. For years I have been telling my patients, 'you must take better care of yourself or you won't live a quality life. You will die if you don't change your ways.' I look at my tray scene and it really hits home. . .this is how I have been living my life. This tray is so packed and I left no room for me to exist in it. Paula, I get the message loud and clear, and I know what I need to do. I am grateful to you for the opportunity to do this loving thing for myself."

Len and I became close friends after this session and kept in touch. He spent the next three years focused on healing himself through every medical and alternative means he felt guided to use. He did not see any patients during those three years. Being a spiritual and intuitive person, he was well guided on his journey back to health. For the past ten years his tumor has been dormant. Len reduced his patient load by seventy-five percent and has learned to pay attention to his own health needs and not just those of his patients. Occasionally he still takes on too much work. When this happens over an extended period of time his health quickly deteriorates, and Len's body speaks loud and clear. . .and he listens and responds once again with open and attentive care.

Don't Worry Mom, I'm Not Really Dead

Patty had a happy story: A beautiful ranch on several acres surrounded by gorgeous forests, a wonderful marriage, two healthy thriving sons, and a fulfilling life. One day tragedy struck and her life stood still. Her eldest son, age nineteen, was killed suddenly in a car accident. She was in shock for two years. The pain felt overwhelmingly unbearable. Patty turned to alcohol to ease the pain, only it did not truly alleviate the suffering and grief she felt over the sudden loss of her son.

After two years of excessive drinking, she became dependent on alcohol almost to a point of completely crossing into a full blown addiction. Fortunately for her an inner voice, an internal prompting, was urging her to get help, and she was able to listen. As part of a treatment program to help her create a life absent of alcohol she came to me for a session. She had read my brochure beforehand and was curious about the work.

When Patty entered my studio she appeared ready and willing to go on a Sand Play Adventure. She said she had a dream about her deceased son the night before. His favorite song was playing in the dream. Once a month, since his death, the song played on the radio, usually at a time when she felt the most distraught. Whenever the song played she felt his presence. The previous night it was especially strong. . .and she did not know why. She only knew she was looking forward to playing in the sand. . .something she had not done since she was a little girl. With enthusiasm and curiosity she created her scene then shared her first impressions of her Sand Play creation.

> Patty: It has several components. The candle light. . .my dogs
> . . .love of cooking and reading, and travel with my
> family. . .the bunnies in my scene are the family
> together as one. There's my husband and our shared
> love of horses. . .he really misses the "me" I was before
> my son died. . .the ballet figure reminds me of how I
> loved ballet as a teen. Over here is my deep connection
> and love of nature and animals. . .the tiger in the corner
> is laughing—he laughs a lot. The feeling of home is
> extremely strong in my scene. It provides a firm foun-
> dation in my life. Right now I feel the presence of my
> son in the studio. This miniature over here represents
> the drinking I did to numb the pain after my son died.

> Paula: As you tune into the firm foundation of home, what
> does it represent?

> Patty: I am whole, I am back and I have peace. My boy is
> watching over me.

With Patty's permission I assist her to move into a deeper state of awareness with the presence of her son. Her whole body posture shifts and her tone of voice changes and she sheds some tears. Something profound is happening within her. It seems as if Patty's son is with us in the room. I encourage Patty to spontaneously say whatever comes to her awareness. I ask her to allow the words to come from the heart. She hears her son speaking to her.

Patty: He's saying, "I love you mom. I'm here through the music. Remember our dream last night? I said I was coming to see you. . .here I am. Don't worry mom, I'm not dead. Once a month I play my favorite song on the radio while you are driving to remind you I'm with you. That's me mom."

Patty: (A serious tone enters into her voice.) I hear my son also saying: "Mom what the hell are you doing? You have to stop this drinking thing you do." I know my son is pleased that I'm getting help but he's not happy with the choices I have made in the past two years He wants me to pay attention...what I do to myself makes a difference, especially to my husband and his younger brother.

Paula: Specifically what does your son want you to pay attention to in your life?

Patty: He tells me to be present every moment. There's nothing you can do about yesterday and you can't rely on tomorrow. . .it hasn't yet happened. So you have to do the best you can with every breath, in every moment . . .like the butterfly. He's saying to me, "Remember mom. . .how you always used to say the butterfly is in 'a state of perfection, doing what they are supposed to be doing. They live moment to moment, beautiful and graceful with every flap of their wings.' Mom that's who you are...'beautiful and graceful.' Be in the moment and you will feel my love more. The pain you feel will lessen. You've got to stop this 'drinking thing.' It changes who you are. (Patty starts to cry again but this time they are tears of joy and release.)

I encourage Patty to work with the butterfly energy through journaling and meditation to help her practice being in the moment. Patty continues talking about the figures in her tray scene.

Patty: The crystals are a source of quiet strength, inspiration and creativity. . .something to explore and work with. When I look at the lion I feel my inner strength and power. It feels like everything in my life is coming together again. I feel my old self coming back, but improved. . .I'm stronger and clearer about who I am.

Patty: (She explores the crystals and their message regarding inspiration and creativity.) I'm feeling an urge to be of service to others instead of focusing on my grief. I want to give more. The message I'm hearing from the crystals is to search for new ways to express my creativity through art, writing. . .let the feelings out and not be afraid to express them. Do not limit myself to what I know now. . .keep opening up to other possibilities.

Paula: What does the lion say?

Patty: I may look like a beast but I am the whole of everything you are trying to put together. . . a body wanting to be healthy and whole again with strength of mind and a spiritual presence of being. The lion tells me his strength is within me.

Paula: What activities will support your desire to become whole again?

Patty: First I want to go sailing. I love the sound of the ocean and its vastness. One can look in every direction and not see anything but openness, clearness, expansiveness and vulnerability. This is a spiritual experience for me. Then there is flying. . .I have frequent flying dreams. The sound and feeling of air blowing through my hair gives me a sense of lightness, agility and flexibility. I'm going to explore taking skydiving lessons when I return home. Then there is the motorcycling. When I sit on the back of a motorcycle it's the closest I come to duplicating my flying dreams. (Patty pauses.) I hear my son say, "Right on mom. All roads lead back home." It's all there in the in the tray. Now I know why I was so eager to play in the sand. My son was planning to be with me during the session.

Over the next year I heard that Patty was doing well and had not returned to drinking.

I'm on a Mission to Solve a Great Mystery

Davis was a psychologist in his mid-forties working in the field of drug and alcohol rehabilitation. His clientele consisted of people who were trying to put an end to their addictions. Now he had to face dealing with his own drug and alcohol addiction. He was in treatment for these problems and doing a Sand Play session was one of his stops to recovery. After we did the clearing process and set the intent for the session, Davis created his scene and participated in the facilitation.

Davis's First Impression of His Tray Scene

Davis: It's dismal and I feel an increasing sense of sadness and depression. My life is in two halves. . .my happy childhood until age eight. . .and from 8 to 23 my totally miserable life.

Paula: Are there any figures in your scene which make you feel inspired or happy?

Davis: The Athena figure. . .it feels both male and female. When I feel the female part I can sense my emotions.

Paula: What do you feel when you tune in to her?

Davis: A longing for beauty, grace. . .she's modest. . . (Davis shifts attention)...the mice in the scene make me happy.

Paula: What about the mice make you happy?

Davis: Mice are cartoon characters. . .remind me of early childhood. They are also my Totem Animal. (Davis refers to power animals in Native American lore.) They bring in lightness for me. When I tune in, I hear them saying something. . .the voice seems distant and tiny. I feel cut off and disconnected and yet something is stirring and it's very uncomfortable.

We discussed this "stirring." It was a new experience for Davis and he had fear around exploring its significance. The mice trigger something deep and painful in him. . .emotions that have been buried a long time. Sensing his discomfort I asked him to select something from the studio collection to help him feel empowered. He selected a fake $1,000,000 bill, however, this did not seem to help Davis feel empowered.

Davis: It's a quick ticket out of my misery. . .More memories are surfacing from the past, between ages 8 and 23, that are painful. I'm back there in time. . .the tray scene feels so real.

Davis shifted his attention to other items in his tray scene. . .a baby and a snake. He put the baby in the mouth of the snake and placed them in the tray.

Davis: I feel something is trying to devour me. . .it foreshadows everything in my life.

I asked Davis if he would like to release all the misery and pain in his tray. He said yes and I asked him what it would take to allow him to do this. He picked up a boy figure off the shelf. He states, "The boy is 14 years old."

Paula: What does he want to do right now? How does he want to feel?

Davis: He wants to feel confident and good about himself.

Paula: What would allow him to do this?

Davis walked around the tray holding the boy figure in his hand and decided to remove all the items in his tray scene. He told me that the boy only wanted mountains and an ocean in his scene. I encouraged him to recreate his world in the sand tray in the way the boy wants. He became totally focused and content, creating his new world as if he were a boy of fourteen.

Paula: How's that feeling?

Davis: I'm not feeling so stilted and stuck anymore. My world feels like it has more potential.

(Davis continued to gather more miniatures for his new scene.)

Davis: This is looking more promising.

Paula: What does the boy see in his new world?

Davis: It's kinda neat. . .it's intriguing. Over there it's striking
. . .there's something mysterious. I'm into sci-fi. This
bridge is from a different world. It's smooth, the curves
are graceful, the color blends. . .a nice combination of
harmony and contrast. . .very interesting!

As Davis talked about his new world his voice softened and he
sounded much younger and full of excitement and curiosity. This was
a very different person from when he first began his session.

Davis: Everything in my world is worth examining. . .the pyramid over here intrigues me. . . it's another mystery to
be explored.

Davis talks about natural beauty and the Lord of the Rings. I
assist him to move deeper into his present experiences.

Paula: Allow yourself to experience and communicate with
the power of your creation. The excitement, the
curiosity, the joy of exploring the mysteries present.
You created this world for yourself. It was a choice you
made. Allow yourself to celebrate its creation.

Davis: (Expresses with great enthusiasm) The crystal next to
the pyramid is close to the world of thoughts but it is
also organic and coming out of the natural world. Over
here this Paleolithic item is from a civilization of long
ago. Wherever I go in my tray scene it's rewarding and
stirs my imagination.

Paula: What's different in this sand tray from the earlier tray scene you did?

Davis: Here I allowed myself to create a world that is fulfilling, interesting, thought provoking at a deep level, in whatever direction I go. I actively released the old and made a decision to find a better symbol for myself. This empowers me and creates a world of intrigue and interest.

Paula: This is what you did.

Davis: Everything feels so different inside of me than when I first came to you. I feel so much more hopeful and this heaviness that was trying to devour me and swallow me whole. . . (Davis refers to the baby in the mouth of the snake). . .has disappeared. I have lived with this feeling for years. In large part that's why I drank and used drugs so much. The high I received was intended to replace the pain I was feeling, only they were taking over my life and swallowing me whole. For the first time in several years I feel there is hope and I have choice.

Paula: You allowed yourself an opportunity to recreate your world even in the midst of misery and pain. The boy in you wanted the freedom to create his world as he saw it. The pain and misery did not allow that boy a chance to do this. Now you have given him expression and let him show you another way of being in the world.

Commentary: Davis left the session with a huge smile on his face that said, "I'm on a secret mission to solve a great mystery. . .and I can't wait to discover what I find."

I worked one more time with him in a group workshop I facilitated. He continued the work from his first session during the workshop, discovering that the great mysteries in life that excited him the most were those hidden within the vast unknown of his own psyche. He no longer needed drugs and alcohol to numb the pain and misery that once overwhelmed his life. He was on a new adventure. . .allowing the curious fourteen year-old within to explore the untapped regions of his mind – beyond the suffering years of ages 8 to 23. Davis was no longer emotionally stuck in this time frame.

He returned to his counseling work as a psychologist following his six-month sabbatical. His focus was to take his work to a whole new level of depth and meaning. The desires to find new purpose in his work, and have it become more soul and heart centered, guided him. He said the explorations he did in the sand tray helped him realize a new realm of possibilities in the counseling field.

It's About Love, Not Fear

Reverend Marion was a colleague "extraordinaire." She worked miracles with people of all ages, from all life backgrounds, who sought her help. Her clarity, wisdom and "no nonsense" therapeutic approach reached them in ways others could not—touching their souls with a presence of heart. I first met her in person when she came to do a sand tray journey in my studio. Previously she had heard about my work through a friend and decided, even before meeting me in person, to send clients from her healing intensives to experience Sand Play as part of their retreat with her. A few months after I began facilitating sessions for her clients, I met Marion in person for the first time. She came in to create a sand tray scene. What a delight it was! After that session, as the months and years rolled by, I was fortunate and blessed to continue working with a number of her clients.

Marion did deep mental, emotional, and spiritual counseling work with people from various parts of the country. When you participated in the Reverend's healing intensive you worked hard and with full conviction. One of the mottos of her healing retreats was, "I am far more than ego tells me." By the time you finished her intensives, you came out a whole new person. You went deeply within, cleared the buried fears holding you back from experiencing love and happiness, and recreated your life script. The journeys I facilitated in the sand tray for Marion's clients were always exciting and interesting. My heart leapt for joy and celebration at the discoveries they made during their Sand Play Adventures. These folks were fully present and willing to dialogue with their soul within the first fifteen minutes of their journey. Once they consciously connected with that place—beyond, ego's grasp—the clients fully embraced what was revealed to them through their sand tray scenes. After they left the studio, with their permission, I would call Marion to fill her in on the session. These after-session discussions were as powerful and uplifting for the two of us as the session itself was to the client.

Communications between my colleague and me were pure and alive with truth, and the depth of information given and received far surpassed what I had previously thought two professionals could share. In the process of supporting and helping our clients in joint alliance, we took our work to a whole new level. We taught each other in ways I have yet to experience with other colleagues. All my exchanges with the beautiful, heartfelt Reverend reinforced my faith.

Both she and I knew: When we operate from a place of Spirit/Soul and Heart mountains of pain, suffering and sadness can be released in a matter of minutes. Once we recognize the truth—the full story of what is really going on—we are given choice.

Marion consistently told me the information I shared with her about the Sand Play sessions with her clients was of immense help, often offering the missing pieces she needed to best assist them. Our insights and observations always complemented, clarified and enhanced our respective work with these clients. Whenever she and I spoke we felt total trust, and had the deepest respect for each other as people and professionals.

Marion's Heart Speaks

Meeting Marion in person for the first time five years before, while facilitating her in the sand tray, had been an absolute delight. Her eyes glowed with warmth and radiance and she had a huge smile on her face the entire session. Her tray scene was colorful and exuded much peace. Her mission statement in life was: "I choose to live my life in peace. Whatever does not bring me peace I choose to not do."

During the facilitation process we explored in depth the significance of a clown marionette she had placed in her tray scene. It had a specific message for her: "Marion, your mission of living in peace is a beautiful journey to take. There is one piece missing you need to include in your daily life that you have not allowed lately. You have been far too serious and have not taken the time to laugh and have fun. Laughter is a joy that brings you peace and you have not been allowing this into you life enough. It's time."

Hearing these words from within she knew her spirit had spoken. In silence she contemplated what her inner voice had said in a serious, self-reflecting manner. I have to admit at that point I too was being very serious. A few moments later the clown marionette suddenly toppled over in her tray. It took us totally by surprise. . .there from the sand bed, in the center of the tray scene, was the clown's smiling face looking up at us with his head tilted to the side as if saying to us both, "Now see! That's funny! That's what this is really about." We burst into laughter. And for five years no matter how intense or serious our conversations became, a healthy dose of laughter always accompanied our discussions. I would describe things (Paula style), of what I saw and felt, and at the other end of the phone line there would be the Reverend cracking up in laughter. Then I would burst out laughing. Marion's laughter was so infectious I had to laugh even when I didn't know what was so funny.

Laughter is food for the soul, and one of the greatest gifts given to humanity. . .and Marion knew how to laugh even during her greatest life challenge. Without warning, she discovered she had a huge cancerous growth on her lungs. With tubes from her chest attached to machines helping her breathe, and causing her tremendous pain and discomfort. . .even then, Marion knew how to laugh!

Five years into our professional relationship and friendship, I was to have one of the most profound encounters with my dear friend when I went to visit her in the hospital. A strong urging within my heart and my soul said, "You must bring your mini sand tray and certain miniatures with you when you see her. I will tell you which ones you need to bring."

Much to Marion's tremendous shock the cancerous tumor invading her lungs was growing significantly larger with each passing day. Only a week before she had entered the hospital with no idea why she had been so tired for the past month and had such difficulty walking. When her daughters took her to the hospital, the doctors were shocked by what they found. The tumor was huge and they could not believe she had functioned as well as she did, for as long as she had. They felt certain she could die at any moment.

When she first talked with me by phone Marion had given up on life. She was far more shocked than the doctors and could not believe what was happening to her body. When I told her I wanted to bring my sand tray and some miniatures her weakened voice instantly became stronger. She responded, "That would be so wonderful. I can't wait. I want to know what is going on with my body. Please bring something blue, pink, and something for my dog, and whatever else you want to bring."

Two days later when I went to visit Marion at the hospital, I barely recognized her. I had not seen her in several months although we had spoken by phone a number of times. When I first arrived she was fast asleep. In a matter of seconds she stirred as she felt my presence in the room. She opened her eyes and smiled and said, "It's time for me to do a sand tray."

Spirit Speaks to Marion in the Sand Tray

The time had come. Present at this session were Marion, the mini tray, some selected miniatures, me. . .and assistance from the Divine that she referred to as Spirit. Marion was a huge fan of Spirit. . .that sacred essence she knew lived and breathed throughout all of existence. **"We are bodies living in Spirit," she would often say, "Not a spirit living in a body.** We only need to awaken to who we truly are and embrace that truth. It's all about Love not Fear." I could not disagree with Marion. I have always felt we are far more than what appears to be. . .and when we connect with our *knowing place* and hear the voice of Soul we become privy to this essence. . .a life force existing and flowing through all that is. Words do not do justice to this infinite aspect of existence. Both she and I felt there is Love and Fear. This is a simplified version of humanity's expression in the world. I also feel there are many shades and variations in between. This was a point of contention between Marion and me. For her it was Love or Fear, and Ego verses Spirit. I was never able to think in such simplistic terms.

An element of my Sand Play work Marion treasured and held in the highest regard was that it provided her clients with opportunities to hear the voice of Spirit in three dimensional form. To witness and experience Spirit through their sand tray scenes brought insight, clarity and wisdom. She felt the Sand Play always complemented and enhanced her work with clients. Marion and I delighted and celebrated when our clients had powerful, life-transforming breakthroughs. She understood as deeply as I the possibilities available to a client when they tap into the immense innate resource of the *knowing place*. And now the moment of truth was facing Marion herself. What was this tumor in her lungs trying to reveal? What was to come next on her life's agenda? Her prognosis looked grim and she knew she needed to make some choices but first she wanted to dialogue with Spirit in the sand tray.

In the hospital a blanket of peace embraced the room. We both felt something profound and magical was about to take place. The nurses, who normally checked on Marion every fifteen minutes, did not enter the room for nearly an hour. Sacred moments ticked away as I experienced one of the most profound Sand Play sessions I have ever facilitated.

Marion slowly opened her eyes a few minutes after I first entered her hospital room. I said, "Here I am. My sandbox and treasures and I are ready to play with you." The "Something blue" Marion asked me to bring, when we spoke by phone, earlier ended up being a figure of a lady wrapped in blue wings folded in a cocoon-like manner, perched on a container holding hidden treasure. The 'something pink' she requested was me, wearing pink pants and a pink rose quartz necklace. "The lady in pink is here to play." I jokingly told her. She smiled her famous smile. I also brought a tiny stuffed plush bunny to represent her dog. Marion and her dog had a deep connection and she felt his immense sadness at not being with her in person. She wanted him to be present with her in the sand tray. I was also guided to bring something to represent our friendship which was two miniature baby dragon figures side by side hugging each other's shoulders. I also brought a newborn angel, the Tibetan Wiseman (later to become The Ancient—one of the Sacred Seven mentioned earlier in the book) and a few other miniatures for Marion to choose in which to create her tray scene.

It took fifteen minutes for Marion to create her tray scene. She became so focused and enamored with the creation process, and the facilitation to follow, that the excruciating pain she felt earlier took a back seat to the Sand Play. Not once did her face or words express the physical suffering she had been enduring. Marion moved into a state of sublime surrender. Deep peace replaced her traumatized state. She was so present and connected to Spirit, and what it wished to share through her sand tray scene, it became one of the easiest sessions I have ever facilitated. I was blessed to witness one of the greatest breakthroughs a person has ever had with me in the sand tray. Marion, a remarkable and gifted counselor and healer for twenty five years, was now on the receiving end of the healing process.

One of the first things she was drawn to was the hugging baby dragons. "Paula, that's you and I healing as one. You and I are in this together. I'm no longer alone. I can ask for help now and you will be with me all the way."

Knowing her as well as I did, I reframed what she said. "That's right Marion; we are joining and healing together as one. We are a team. You are no longer alone. I support whatever choices you make because I know you are guided by Spirit and will make the highest and best choice."

Marion smiled in response and continued to share her innermost thoughts. "This newborn angel is me. . .who I truly am. I am innocent and in total surrender to Spirit and it feels so right and wonderful." Marion started to cry. (It was the first time I ever saw her cry.) She continued, "I could never fully feel my innocence. . .deep down a part of me always felt I was not good enough."

Whenever Marion spoke about her work or herself she expressed strong convictions about what she saw and felt. There were times, however, when she held certain beliefs so strongly no one could convince her differently even if the situation warranted it. Though she was often accurate in her observations about her clients, her friends, and family there were other times when she was not. During those times she became fixated and would not allow for different possibilities, especially when they triggered her own issues. Reaching out and allowing a friend or colleague to assist her when objectivity was needed in dealing with a personal issue was almost nonexistent for Marion. Showing her vulnerability and expressing her fears. . .when they arose. . .happened only on the rarest of occasions.

Today, for the first time, Marion totally surrendered. Her defenses were down and she allowed me to witness all of her. . .not only her strength, wisdom and love, but also her fears, confusion, and extreme vulnerability. She was facing the greatest journey of her life . . .and not just whether she would die or not. . .the greater journey was about Marion realizing who she truly was in the bigger picture of her life. Marion and I were friends and colleagues in the purest sense. That day the love in our hearts was joined as one and we were equals. It was no longer Marion and Spirit verses everyone else. It was Marion, Spirit and me and whoever else she invited. . .sharing a space in life together. **In the place of joining as equals—not "them" versus "I" —Love multiplies in strength many-fold. . .and all is possible.** For Marian it was a huge realization that I truly wanted, and was willing, to share this journey with her, and that I would do so every step of the way. She finally accepted that she was indeed good, worthy and deserving enough, even in her fragile, depleted state. This amazing lady allowed me to enter her world, and not just "the fun, I'm in control and everything is okay" part, but the "I'm afraid, I don't know what's happening, help me find out why" part.

During the facilitation, Marion told more about what the new born angel represented in her scene. "This is who I am. I feel Spirit wanting me to know my innocence. Once I accept this fully (Marion pauses). . .but why am I holding back and not allowing. . .why is this tumor attacking my lungs?" As she said these words she coughed and her breathing became labored. . .it was as if her lungs were saying, "excuse me I have something to say." Marion instantly shifted her attention to the figure standing behind the newborn angel. . .the Tibetan Wiseman. A look of amazement fell over her face. "He's my power. . .I'm afraid to accept my power. Even after all these years doing my healing work and counseling I never felt it was safe to fully reveal myself...something in the background kept saying don't you dare. . .it's not okay to use my gifts fully."

Marion was exceptionally intuitive and had other unique abilities that neither her parents nor their religious beliefs could accept. Marion told me that during her childhood she was placed in a mental institution because her parents thought she was crazy. After extensive testing she was released because the doctors found nothing wrong with her.

I encouraged her to tune into the message of, "something saying, 'don't you dare.'" Marion started to cry from a place of tremendous emotional pain deep inside her. Through the tears she whimpered in agonizing sadness, "I denied the little girl inside of me the right to feel sadness and pain over what happened to me back then. I was never accepted by my father as being okay and deserving of love. I hurt so badly inside because I was different and my father never allowed me the right to hurt. No one comforted me. . .and when I grew up I never allowed me to comfort me or the little girl inside either."

In her adult years Marion had forgiven her parents' inability to understand her unusual abilities. . .to know things before they happened, to see illness in a person's body before it was diagnosed, and to experience other dimensions of reality. She loved her parents, regardless of their fear and non-acceptance of these abilities. In their own way they loved her too, and Marion had made her peace with them, except in one crucial area of her life.

As Marion continued to cry she said, "My father never held me or wiped away my tears when I hurt. It was not okay to feel sad and afraid. As a little girl I was never allowed to be innocent. . .my abilities brought shame to my father and I never let go of that shame. I never felt it was okay to show my pain and hurt." Marion stopped crying. "My daughters, particularly Cassie, will not express their fears, pain or hurt either. They often act like everything is okay, even when it's not —just like their mother. By my own example I have denied my wounded child a right to be heard, held, and healed."

I asked Marion just to be with this internal child for a few moments by holding the baby angel to her heart and loving the wounded child. She did this and started to cry from an even deeper place of pain and hurt. I encouraged her to let it all out. As she did, Marion began to feel the heaviness she had felt on her lungs dissipate and her breathing became easier. She was amazed and grateful. For the first time in days she was not feeling oxygen starved and breathing was not painful.

Marion continued, "Paula, I need to accept my power and abilities fully. I want to allow myself to be the new born angel. . .to experience my innocence fully. I want to be the Wise Ancient Man, and not be afraid of my power. There's something more I need to understand here about him."

I asked, "What does he have to say that you need to understand further?"

Marion responded, "It's time I fully accept my innocence and allow my wounded child to feel safe from harm and let her know it's okay to be cared for when she feels hurt or sad. I never gave her a voice, not really. I feel her inside me now wanting to break free. All I have to do is set her free."

Marion's attention shifted to the lady wrapped in the blue wings. She comments, "She's the lady wrapped in blue wings ready to come out. Paula, I need a few minutes to be alone and process all this. This experience was absolutely profound. I feel so released and much lighter on the inside." I left Marion to be alone for twenty minutes.

When I returned, she told me of further discoveries she'd made. The nurse arrived to take Marion's vitals and asked if she wanted some morphine. Marion said no to the morphine as she did not need it. It was the first time in days she felt no pain. The nurse was surprised. Previously she had been in excruciating pain and now she was feeling fine. The medical staff couldn't help noticing the sand tray and the miniatures placed inside it. The look in their eyes said they were curious but did not dare pry. They attended to Marion's needs and left as quickly as possible. They were respectful of what I was doing and tried to stay out of the room as much as they could. Marion said she overheard the doctors a few days earlier talking and saying they did not understand why she was still alive. In fifteen years of doctoring they had never seen anyone with such a huge tumor in the lung region who was still living.

Soon Marion fell into a deep sleep but first she told me she knew the reason the tumor had suddenly appeared. She had been holding back from fully allowing Love into her life. She realized now that in truth she was perfectly okay, and that she was deserving of love, so there was no longer a need to punish herself. She had done no wrong. She just needed to realize this and allow all of her to be loved. . .and not just the 'okay parts' but the parts of her that felt hurt, afraid or sad. The last few words she said to me before she fell asleep were, "I know everything will be all right now."

Her tumor was there and she had choices to make. Marion felt with certainty she would make the right choice for herself. She would allow herself to move fully into her power and accept her innocence— whatever that meant—because the time was nearing to do so. She felt a huge burden had been lifted off her chest and she was ready to move into her new destiny. . .whether that meant remaining on planet earth or moving on to another dimension.

Marion was not afraid to die. Many times in her life she had traveled to worlds and dimensions beyond ordinary comprehension; and she knew there were wondrous and magnificent realities yet to explore in those vast realms of existence. At the center of it all is Love. . .and anyone who chooses can open to its magnificent power. She had decided she was ready to awaken fully to Love and claim her full power.

I saw Marion one more time that week and talked with her twice by phone. Our conversation centered on what it meant to move beyond what was physically happening to her. She was receiving the medical treatment available to her, and connected with family and friends via phone or in person. There was one more important question Marion wanted to have answered: "What's next for me once I move beyond my present life circumstances?" Marion knew Spirit was helping her to decide. Exactly one week after she did her Sand Play session I tried to call Marion. She had just moved into a hospice home the night before. It was 10:☺o AM (Side note: A happy face just appeared on the screen when I pressed "o" on the key board. . .I cannot pull up a happy face by pressing the zero key. I do not even know of any key that can do this. It has never happened before. . ."Is that you Marion?" I quietly queried. I can't help but think so because she always put a happy face with her signature whenever she sent me notes.)

I called the hospice. A man answered and said he was the priest. "She is busy right now and can't talk. Can you call back in a little while?" I said okay. I sat quietly for twenty minutes, feeling a strange tingling in my body. I knew something profound was happening to Marion. . .but had no idea what it was. I called back and the same man answered. He told me Marion had passed away. The first time I called she had been receiving her last rites and was in the process of transitioning though I did not know this at the time. Somehow, we were connecting in spirit as she was passing into another dimension of reality. It seemed that in her own way she wanted me to be present. After the priest gave me the news I asked to speak to her eldest daughter. When she answered the phone we just cried.

"Beloved Marion you will be missed. In my heart of hearts I know you have chosen well—wherever you are. Thank you for the happy face. . .I know it's time to lighten up and laugh more. . .I have been too serious lately."

It Bites

Kerry, age 10, attempted to commit suicide a few months prior to our session. When I first met her, this highly intelligent, perceptive and sensitive girl was extremely depressed and still suicidal. Reverend Marion had been counseling Kerry's father for a few years and encouraged him to bring the girl to do a Sand Play the next time he and his daughter were visiting from the east coast. Marion wanted to receive some insight into the inner thought processes of Kerry, and felt certain her client's sand tray scene would offer the information needed to help encourage this girl to choose in favor of life. It was to be the first of two sessions I did with her. The second session was with her and her father.

The moment Kerry came into my studio she was mesmerized by the miniatures on my shelves and the sand tray stationed in the center of my studio. She smiled at me and without saying a word proceeded to create her sand tray scene. Once completed, she shared her story about the village, its' people, and their animals. With only a little encouragement she allowed me into her world.

Paula: Hmm, I'm curious. What's your scene about?

Kerry: There's a village and animals. The villagers living there are happy because they have a peaceful life because they have animals.

Paula: Why do the animals make them happy?

Kerry: Because they are spirits.

Paula: What does it mean to have animal spirits?

Kerry: They teach them things.

Paula: What kinds of things?

Kerry: How to live on what they can survive on. What they can eat and things they can grow.

Paula: Is there anything else they teach them about daily living?

Kerry: To live life full. Each person needs their own place and to be given respect. The villagers get along fine. They are healthy and work together in all things. They listen to the animal spirits.

Paula: What is the statue in the middle of the village?

Kerry: It's the spiritual statue. . .It's God. He teaches the people to respect the animals. If you leave them alone, they will leave you alone.

Paula: Do the people in your home get along?

Kerry: No.

Paula: If you were a spirit animal what would you like to see happen in your home?

Kerry: Respect and kindness to others.

Paula: Is there someone in particular who does not get along?

Kerry: Yah, my mom and me.

Paula: How about you and your dad?

Kerry: Yah, we get along.

Paula: What would you like to tell your dad about being at home?

Kerry: It bites.

Paula: What bites?

Kerry: The way we live. My brothers are not nice and they don't give me space. My mom tries to give me space but she always messes it up. She looks in my room, tries to read my diary. I don't have a diary anymore.

Paula: What happened to your diary?

Kerry: I got rid of it because it was no longer private. I have no privacy in my house. I have no place to think and feel and be myself. I do not exist. Kerry does not exist. Only bad feelings and fighting exists in my home but not in the sand tray. In here there is peace and happiness. Everyone gets along and each person can be themselves. Even the animals and people respect and accept each other."

The session was ending and I asked Kerry if I could tell Reverend Marion about the session. She responded, "Yes. I like Marion. She really listens to me. She does weird stuff."

Reverend Marion worked very differently than any healing practitioner or counselor I knew. I did not fully understand how she worked—I only knew she had worked miracles with her clients.

After this session, I met Kerry one more time with her dad. The observations I shared with Marion about Kerry during these sessions gave Marion enough insights that helped her work with the family as a whole unit, so that Kerry decided life was worth living.

Commentary: Kerry and both her older and younger brother were adopted. The parents, though they dearly loved their children, could not get along with each other. Extreme tension and anger carried into the home environment and into their interactions with their children. For Kerry and her older brother—whom I also worked with individually a few months earlier—life at home was like living in a pressure cooker. The older brother became hyperactive and often picked fights with Kerry to release his frustrations. The younger sibling, who I never met, would take his sister's belongings and often destroy them. The father remained passive during the warring episodes between siblings. Her mother always wanted to know what Kerry was doing—continually asking her questions and making demands on her daughter for personal time. Her dad, the more passive of the two parents, did not interact much with his wife unless they had a fight. Then he usually yelled.

After Kerry's attempted suicide, the family went into counseling. Little progress was made until Marion started to work with the entire family. The information I passed on to her about Kerry assisted her with the missing piece.

Being a super-sensitive child, Kerry deeply felt the tension and inner rage brewing between her parents. The mother turned to her daughter for the substitute support and connection she did not feel with her husband. Kerry's brothers lashed out at their sister as a result of their reaction to the parent's friction and tension. They felt the turmoil and intensity generated by the parents and Kerry was the ideal outlet to release their frustration and anger. They had little under-standing of what they were doing; only that something inside them wanted to explode. Their sister was the target. There was no place for Kerry to go to escape the pressure and demands made on her from her mother, the attacks from her brothers, or her father's seeming indif-ference. The young girl felt trapped and could not exist as Kerry. Death did not scare her. She became a non-entity, and the idea of death seemed the only course of action to take.

Fortunately, the information I received from Kerry's tray scene and story, and the older brother's previous session with me, filled in some missing pieces concerning the family's dynamics. As Marion worked with the whole family she could help the parents understand what living at home felt like from their children's point of view. The result was that the parents, who did love their children, took another look at themselves, their actions and the impact their strained, tenu-ous marriage was having on the family unit. Months later Marion said that the family as a whole was doing much better, and Kerry no longer threatened to commit suicide. The parents, still unable to work out the differences in their marriage, were seriously contemplating divorce. Their parenting skills significantly improved and they became more sensitive towards their children. They learned to not burden their children with their problems. They are more aware and therefore more careful not to project their problems and issues concerning each other onto their children.

Shannon's Story

Shannon, an experienced psychotherapist, first came to me for a sand tray session after she was diagnosed with cancer. She wanted to have more clarity and a better understanding as to the emotional and mental dynamics between her and the cancer that was invading her body. Having gone through many years of personal growth, self-discovery, and therapy, along with working as a therapist, Shannon was a seasoned professional. She was no stranger to the hidden agendas and transgressions of the mind and its effect on our emotional and physical bodies. She was also familiar with Sand Play therapy as a therapeutic tool to help heal troubled emotions and dysfunctional thinking patterns. Well liked, and in demand as a therapist, she was a successful career woman.

As a single parent, however, her personal life challenged her to the extreme. Her son had serious environmentally-induced health problems that required continual, specialized care. Unknowingly, Shannon had been exposed to deadly toxins when pregnant. As the only parent raising her son (the father chose not to be part of his son's life) it was Shannon and her boy versus the world. When it came to her health she paid close attention. If something happened to her, her son Jeffery age 11, would have no one. Her own father was dead, her relationship with her mother was exceptionally strained, and her only brother was also ill with cancer. When Shannon came for her sand tray session she wanted to learn what was going on in her body and her role in what was happening. Shannon was a firm believer in "mind over matter" and did not subscribe to the idea that allopathic medicine was the only way to heal the body. She believed in alternative medicine and had decided to work with both approaches. Her only goal was to get well and raise Jeffrey into adulthood. I did two individual sessions with Shannon. Here are the highlights of those two journeys.

First Session

After we did a clearing ritual to calm the mind, and set the intent for the session, Sharon gathered her miniatures and created her tray scene. I then asked her: "Observe the world you have created. Allow whatever thoughts, feelings and impressions to come silently to the surface. You are communing with your creation. When you feel ready, walk around the tray and look at your scene from different angles. See if any information changes. You may add, take away or shift any item in your tray, if you wish. When you have come full circle the facilitation will begin."

After allowing Shannon time for inner reflection we proceeded to explore the significance of the world she created.

Paula: What is your first impression of the world you created?

Shannon: The center of my scene marks a journey. . .it's back and forth, and it's retracing itself. . .it's not far from home. It affects everything I do. Over in this corner it feels like the desert and hills. The other corner feels dark and locked up (she refers to the castle and a half buried figure next to it). . .it brings up a lot of pain. The figure may represent the pain. . .I kinda try to bury. A lot of the figures I picked seem to be wise figures of wisdom and depth. That figure over there reminds me of me. He's my "Tigger*". I always liked him. To me he has bravado and assurance. Behind him is another wise figure to remind me I have depth. The figure here is Native American and I chose to have her facing away from everything in the scene. . .I see her going off, away from everyone . . .It's supposed to be that way. The tiny blue crystal in the middle is so beautiful I had to set it apart. I want to get there but I can't seem to. The crystal skull in my scene is part of the journey affecting me. It's the end point. (*Tigger is a cartoon character from the children's book "Winnie the Pooh.")

Earlier Shannon had said, "That figure reminds me of me. He's my 'Tigger.' I've always liked him. To me he has bravado and assurance." Since this piece she calls 'Tigger' is a positive and empowering image for Shannon, I felt guided to bring him into the story early and to call upon his energy to act as a voice from her *knowing place*. I sensed we were about to enter a delicate zone in her thinking process and that she might need all the strength and support we could muster.

Paula: What does the figure representing Tigger say about this?

Shannon: He makes me think of my mother.

Paula: Would you like to know more about that?

Shannon: Yes.

Paula: How do you feel about what's going on in your tray scene?

Shannon: It feels good. . .like I've done a good job, I feel competent.

Paula: Is there one figure you're most drawn to at this time?

Shannon: Fox draws me in the most right now.

Paula: What is the significance of the fox energy? What does he say about this journey you are on?

Shannon: There's a sense of cunning and secretiveness. He says I'm hiding something from myself.

We explore deeper into the fox's secret—what's hidden in Shannon and wanting to be revealed. In the back of my mind I am prepared to bring in the symbolism of Tigger and what he represents to her should the need arise, if she needs extra support.

Paula: Check within and see if this secret would be willing to reveal itself. . .if so, what happens when you ask about the secret, what does it say?

Shannon: It's me. I suspect there is a relationship between. . .

Shannon is becoming analytical. . .something we therapists are very good at doing. . .so I intercede. I want her to be present with her experience from her feeling base, not the intellect. I ask her to move her energy from her head into her heart and imagine herself breathing in and out from the heart region. As she does this Shannon quickly moves into a more heightened state of awareness.

Paula: What is the secret willing to share?

Shannon: It has to do with my mother. It's about how to be "me" when I am in my mother's presence. . .Fox helps me to get away or hide.

Paula: Ask fox if this way of detaching from your mother is a healthy way that's right for you?

Shannon: He says do what I need to and let the chips fall where they may but don't hide.

Paula: Anything else he would like to share?

Shannon: Foxes, when they come out, they show themselves briefly and then they're gone. He tells me I don't have to do it all at once. He wants me to change how I interact with my mother. . ."Go for it," he says, "but not too fast." Being honest in my mother's presence is the challenge. I think fox is right. Changing how I interact with my mother, slowly and gradually, will protect, not destroy our relationship.

Next Shannon explores the significance of a figure she placed in her scene who she perceives as Guinan (a character from television series Star Trek: The Next Generation.) In the TV series this character witnessed her people and their planet being destroyed. She was the only one of her kind who survived the obliteration of her race. Shannon was drawn to this figure because of the wisdom she feels the character exudes. In the television series Guinan is a wise woman highly regarded by the crew of the USS Enterprise. The symbolism of what this character represents to Shannon is empowering her.

Paula: What does the figure representing Guinan say to you about what you just said?

Shannon: (Sidetracking.) Mom is so anxious. . .honesty with her can provoke more anxiety in her and I don't want to cause the anxiety.

Paula: How would Guinan respond to what you've said?

Shannon: Honesty is how we are going to rebuild the relationship. I can't protect her from her anxiety. I need to tap into the deepest part of me and speak from that place of wisdom.

Paula: Ask Wisdom how to use this knowing to get past your fear and speak your truth.

Shannon: She says to pick my battles.

Paula: What do you mean?

Shannon: Tune in to whatever is resonating most deeply with me at the time.

Paula: How can you get in touch with this?

Shannon: It's a solar plexus thing, a feeling just below my rib cage. Breathing helps expand it and to feel what's really right and true for me.

Paula: Have you been practicing this?

Shannon: Yes, what would be new is to do it when I'm interacting with my mom.

Commentary: When we make a change within ourselves, how deeply that change is experienced and integrated into our daily lives is often put to the test by the people who tend to trigger us the most —our family. For Shannon, it is her mother.

Paula: Ask the wise person you refer to as Guinan, "How can I move through the challenge with mom with greater ease?"

Shannon: She says, "Use my breathing to stay centered."

Paula: Is there anything else this wise person wants you to know right now?

Shannon: She says, "Meditation." (Suddenly her attention diverts to the miniature of "Tigger" His energy and his significance to Shannon in her tray scenes seems be interceding.)

Paula: What does he want to say?

Shannon: You can do it, you can be it. Lighten up, don't get bogged down. Keep smiling. . .say the truth and keep smiling.

Paula: Ask him how can you pull that smile out of you when you don't feel it?

Shannon: Have that attitude. . ."It's that Tiggerness. . .taking the solid stance, putting my hands on my hips and straighten up my posture. . .breathe and just do that Tiggerness thing!"

Paula: I suggest you work with this energy on a daily basis, or whenever you need it. Breathe him in, take that posture with that attitude and let it out. . .that truth, whatever it is in that moment, and give it a voice. . .

Shannon: I'm putting my hands on my hips and doing "that thing". . ."Telling it like it is."

Commentary: The figure many refer to as Tigger is a character often used in the sand tray among my clients. The image he represents stirs them into action. His "doingness" and confidence, coupled with what they often call the "Tigger stance" has brought smiles to many people have who played with him during their Sand Play experience.

Shannon's attention next moves to the "Native American Princess" located in an area of the tray she called the wasteland. The figure is looking in a specific direction. Knowing Shannon's history, and that she has spent a number of years working on her own issues, I felt she was strong enough to enter the wasteland. My intuition said it was in this place Shannon would learn the important information she needed to know about the cancer invading her body. She was ready to enter the wasteland in her scene knowing she could stop the exploration at any time, should it become necessary. Sand Play is intended to be a very respectful and sensitive process when dealing with the needs of clients.

Paula: What is the Native American Princess looking at?

Shannon: She's looking out into the horizon. . .she's wanting to go out there...she's wanting to flee.

Paula: What does she want to flee from?

Shannon: She wants to leave the wasteland, this featureless expanse—it seems to be a good thing, but I have mixed feelings about it.

Paula: Allow yourself to flow into the featureless expanse— just be with it with no expectation or need for it to be anything, it just is. . .just allow yourself to be in this place and to feel it. . .(I give Shannon several moments to experience the featureless expanse) . . .now come back and let this place tell you whatever it wishes to share. How do you feel?

Shannon: It hurts, I can feel it tighten my throat and impact my breathing. I can see a flat desert with a dead tree and the princess standing out there with her hair blowing.

Paula: Would you be willing to place the figure who represents Wisdom, the one you call Guinan, in the middle of the wasteland? (Shannon places this miniature there without hesitation.) To explore the energy of the wasteland in more depth maybe your "Tigger"—with his assurance and bravado would like to join in as well. (Shannon eagerly moves him into the wasteland.)

Paula: What is happening for you, Shannon, now that these two figures have entered the wasteland to be with the princess?

Shannon: (Sidetracking.) We're standing in the sand and it's like devastation. There were buildings and playgrounds. . .now they're gone and covered with sand. (I move with Shannon's conscious flow wherever she needs to go in the scene.)

Paula: Is it a past or future feeling?

Shannon: Past. . .the feeling that comes from childhood.

Paula: Has this feeling of devastation been with you for awhile or is this a new feeling?

Shannon: It's old, but being covered with sand is new.

Paula: What does Guinan say about that?

Shannon: That there was a lot of devastation.

Paula: Does the buildings being covered with sand say anything to you?

Shannon: It's like a ghost town—in the past.

Paula: Is the same thing existing now or is it a past feeling invading your present situation?

Shannon: When Guinan came with me it felt removed, it doesn't hurt.

Commentary: It seems as though Shannon's entire identity and sense of beingness is trapped in the wasteland and it's taking every ounce of her strength to survive, and be there for her son. She has strong inner resources that help her endure the challenges she must face; however, I sense there is something deep within her asking to be heard. When it surfaces it will be a significant key to unlocking the mysteries surrounding her present bout with cancer. The discovery of this key was not to be today as the session needed to draw to an end. Two hours had passed and I could sense Shannon's exhaustion. To pursue this exploration further at this time would be counter-productive and risky, given her present health.

Whenever a client is on the verge of a breakthrough and it's at the very end of a session I encourage the client to return for a follow-up session as soon as possible. Shannon had taken the first crucial steps in her discovery process. The next phase of the journey was yet to come. . .but she was eager. I brought the session to a close by making the following suggestion.

"Shannon, when the feeling of devastation, hurt and tightness arises in your throat, call in the energy of wisdom you tuned into when we explored the significance of Guinan. Allow yourself to be in the 'now' place with this wise energy flowing through you. Breathe in her wisdom and let it expand. Breathe out any constriction you may be feeling. Ask her for guidance to help you work through these intense emotions. . .and bring in that attitude you refer to as the 'Tiggerness Attitude' to lighten things up a little."

Second Session

Shannon came in for a follow-up session three months later. In between I did one session with her son, and one with Shannon and her son. (She also had the surgery to remove the cancerous growth in her throat. She was awaiting the test results.)

Working with Shannon's son individually, and doing a mother/son session, helped empower them both. Jeffery, an exceptionally bright and creative boy, had a great time playing in the sand tray. Connecting with his mother in this way allowed him to work through some of their issues. Jeffery was annoyed with his mom because she did not spend as much time with him as he would have liked.

Shannon had been working two jobs to pay the bills. When she had the surgery, and needed to recuperate afterwards, her time with her son was restricted. Any free time she had was always spent with him. Jeffery's sand tray creation revealed he was very concerned about his mother's health. He was afraid she would die. Shannon was far from dying. (The cancer was localized.) Still, Jeffery needed a lot of reassurance.

With all this going on, Shannon was more determined than ever to understand the hidden forces within herself that contributed to her present health challenges. As soon as she entered the studio for her second individual session, she spontaneously and quickly created her tray scene—fully ready and willing to find out the story behind her cancer and what it wanted. Health wise, she was feeling better and stronger. . .and she was in better spirits than in the previous individual session.

First Impression of Her Tray Scene

Shannon: The paint brushes and rocking horse are about play and having fun, I feel I'm being sent on a journey . . .and there's the emergence. . .my spiritual guides are present in the tray. The figure with the large green eyes...maybe the cancer...he's homely. There's also a lot of beauty in my scene. . .the flowers and trees feel protecting. . .I feel a merging of wisdom and courage coming together.

Paula: Do any feelings come up at this moment as you talk about your scene?

Shannon: I don't like that thing there. . .it's like a part of me— but not a part of me. . .it's like the cancer. . .I wish it would go away. . . and yet his big green eyes are sort of endearing. . .maybe even transmuting. . .I look at this strange homely face and I feel there may be more going on than I see. (We explore these feelings and observations in greater depth.)

Shannon: The figure has a strange message.

Paula: Why don't you dialogue with the green-eyed figure? If you feel okay to do so, look into his eyes. Allow those eyes to speak to you in any manner you feel comfortable.

Shannon: He's a figure with opposing energies. I hate him yet he's endearing. . .there's innocence about him in his homeliness. I want him gone yet he's part of me. I know he has a message. There exists a commonality where opposition has a common ground of agreement. This is important. . .

Paula: Allow the commonality to speak to you.

Shannon: The cancer is of my own body. . . it's me. . .and it's gone wrong. . .it has a mixed quality. It is a part of me, but gone wrong. . .it's like Gollum—that character from Lord of the Rings. It has opposing elements like the cancer.

Paula: Let's try dialoguing with these two sides of the cancer. . ."it's part of me" and "it's a part that has gone wrong."

It's Part of Me

Shannon: It's a messenger. It has gotten stronger and wants to be heard. . .it's a part of me I don't allow. . .it's just wanting to be accepted as no better or worse than any other part. . .it's in the dark and can't see.

Paula: Does it want to see?

Shannon: Yes, it wants to be seen and acknowledged. . .there's a beauty and simplicity. . .it has a beauty in it's simplicity. . .it just is. . .the raw truth. . .it can be beautiful.

Paula: What's the raw truth?

Shannon: I need to be out of the box. . .I need to express. . .I need to be allowed. Sometimes I get caught up in the business of fear. It seems easier to not express myself and avoid the fear. . .it seems easier, but it's not.

Paula: What does the raw truth say about this?

Shannon: It's me squished when I don't let the expression out.

Paula: Let's check in with the part that's gone wrong.

The Part that's Gone Wrong

Shannon: It's thwarted, squished, suppressed. . .it's so distorted. It's going down the wrong path because it can't go down the right path. . .it's not happy because it hasn't been allowed to be.

Paula: What wants to be allowed?

Shannon: It wants all my feelings and expressions to be allowed. When it gets channeled into this distorted form, it's not allowed. It's too powerful to stop.

Paula: What's too powerful to stop?

Shannon: The expression needs to be expressed. . .I've not done it. . .cancer is the result.

Paula: Does this side "gone wrong" agree with what you've said about being squished?

Shannon: It has to be squished, although it would prefer to be expressed, however, if I want to squish "me" down, I will be squished down.

Paula: (Summarizing what Shannon said.) The cancer is doing what it is doing and you are being squished. You deny your expression, it rebels and says no. If you are going to squish me, I will rebel more. (She nods in agreement.)

Paula: From the place of "raw truth" who or what is the cancer and what does it want?

Shannon: It's me and my need to express and be acknowledged by me.

Paula: Tune in and see what the wisdom of the raw truth wants to share about this expression within wanting to be acknowledged by you. . .

The characters that represented Tigger and Guinan to Shannon in her first tray scene are present this time as well. A feather she placed in her scene enters the story now. When she listens, it says it wants her to be who she is, and not what she thinks she's supposed to BE. "Take the gloves off and just "BE," is the internal message she hears.

Shannon: Guinan has the wisdom, Tigger has the courage, and now I just need to breathe and show up. The trees are poetry of nature. . .it's another expression. . .I love to be out in nature. I see things in the form of poetry. . . the beauty, the flowers. . .unlocking the simplicity. . . I have difficulty keeping things simple.

I make everything so complicated and it weighs me down.

Paula: How does simplicity want to be brought out in your life at this time?

Shannon: Reduce the clutter in my house, keep flowers in my crystal bowl, follow my intuition, let my intuition guide me. . .don't seize up. I get this tension in my body. . .I need to breathe and not let my head intervene. . .breathe and let my intuition flow.

Paula: When your head gets involved, what does raw truth say?

Shannon: Be Tigger, do and say what you need to say. Turn to my spirit guides. . .focus on them instead of the tension and mind activity. The rocking horse is about play. . .I need to play more. Brushes are about drawing and painting. . . I love to draw and paint. I've not allowed myself to do this. . .it's time to paint and draw. The journey. . .the crystal path with the color gems on it are leading to the figure with the large green eyes. . .it's about expansion. . .it allows me to open that part of me that was closed. Being closed down resulted in cancer. . .it was me crying out, begging me to open up to myself. The turtle in the shell is me unlocking, coming out of my shell. Dolphins remind me also to play more and write my stories. . .then there is the cloaked figure.

Paula: What does the cloaked figure say about all that you have said?

Shannon: Yes to it all. . .this whole scene. . .the message in the tray. How can I deal with all of this? It's a lot right now. The cloaked figure says, "Don't worry about time. Just allow and all will open in a timely fashion. 'Just be aware and ask,' I hear him say. "Don't push the flow. Let it organically express in its own natural timing."

Paula: What does the angel off to the side of your scene say about this?

Shannon: She says, "see the beauty you seek, right there before in your life. It's evolving and growing. Decrease the clutter in your life. Allow room for the beauty and simplicity to enter your personal space. I can help you with this."

Paula: Guess what Shannon, there is no devastation in this tray scene. This is very different than the scene you created the first time. What happened?

Shannon: The devastation was me squishing me. Now my suppressed self is being allowed expression. She is moving into peace, beauty, freedom. . .in alignment with my highest self/creator/universe. I'm not hiding or denying myself. I'm letting my cancer show me the truth. I will no longer hold back my expression.

Commentary: In the months following this session Shannon continued to allow herself to open up through creative expression. . . writing, drawing and painting. She went on fun dates with friends and learned to say no to those activities that caused complications in her life. She sold a lot of her personal possessions, simplifying life significantly for herself and her son. She started to speak more truthfully with her mother. After her brother died of cancer, Shannon decided to change careers so she could earn more money in less time. Spending more time with her son, pursuing personal activities that are fun and creatively expressive became top priorities in her life. Her periodic check-ups indicated she was still cancer-free. She found the secret to being healthy, happy, and whole. . .the self-assured and bravado qualities in her personality she now calls her, "Tiggerness" holds the key. Last I heard she and her son were living in Maine. Both were happy and doing well.

What Would You Do if You Could Talk to the Cows?

Callie was a writer in her mid-fifties. She did one session, after being referred to me as part of a treatment program designed to help her with a drinking problem. The focus was on helping her come to terms with areas in her life that were causing her much stress. For the most part, her life read like a happy story, however, something significant was missing for Callie. She felt Sand Play could help discover what it was. Shortly after she arrived we did the clearing and set the intent for the session. Then she created her tray scene with quiet inward resolve and the desire to understand herself better. This is a condensed version of what unfolded during the facilitation.

Paula: What is your first impression of the world that you created?

Callie: It's a home environment that seems to have everything I need.

Paula: As you walked around your tray scene does anything else surface?

Callie: I didn't like the two plastic items I put in, and I keep wondering why the Native American Indian is in my scene.

Paula: Do any feelings come up for you?

Callie: I feel pleasure, I see a lot of possibilities and I feel I should be excited but I don't know if I am.

Paula: What are you most drawn to in the tray?

Callie: The woman at the head of the bridge in the center of my scene. I'm surprised I picked up the bridge.

Paula: Why?

Callie: It seems to fit. My partner and I have a lake on our ranch but there is no bridge on our property. I don't know why I picked it.

We explore the area with the bridge and woman thoroughly. Callie is strongly drawn to this area and I follow up by questioning her in-depth. The woman at the head of her bridge is an exotic-looking figure holding a crystal ball extended outward on her right arm. She is standing on an island. She is draped in chic robes and looking at her crystal. On her other extended arm perched on her hand is an eagle. The woman is poised and ready for action. She's facing away from the bridge and does not see the little woman at the other end with clenched fists trying to get her attention.

Callie: She says, "I'm holding this beautiful world in my hand. Look how graceful I am. This could be you if you get your 'shit' together."

Paula: What shit are you referring to?

Callie: Being confident in my writing. . .letting go of self-doubt, just do it and don't worry about why I'm writing, or the outcome.

Paula: Does she offer you a way how to do this?

Callie: She tells me, "Look toward the world and keep your focus on whatever is there and be truthful." My inner reality is heavier than the outer but it's not unpleasant . . .it's comfortable.

Paula: Bring "you" into the equation of writing. Where do you fit into the scheme?

Callie: On the other side of the bridge is an island with a little woman on it clenching her fists. She's trying to get my attention. She's saying, "ENOUGH!"

Paula: Enough of what?

Callie: Tension and anger. . .

Paula: What else does she say?

Callie: In caring so much about what the exotic woman wants she can't let things flow.

Paula: What does the exotic woman want?

Callie: She wants me to take my inner reality and put it out there in the world. And the little woman is saying don't let go. Don't give yourself away. Don't get caught up and be so fixed on what's in the outer world. Focus on what's inside you.

Paula: Therein lays the duality. What would it take to relax the conflict?

Callie: She needs to turn and face the bridge but she's feeling apprehensive.

Paula: What will help her take the next step?

Callie: Humor. . .there has to be humor and it has to be big for her to go over the bridge.

Paula: What would make it big enough for her to cross the bridge?

Callie: It has to be loud. She needs to move around. Maybe she should be on the bridge and not wait for something to happen.

Paula: Maybe she would like to be closer to the woman who wants to go with the flow without tension and anger.

Callie: Yah. . .she really wants that. . .now she is drawn to the bridge and wants to reach for what is on the other side. I think she needs more humor in her life.

Callie moves the colorful bus filled with happy people from the corner of her tray scene to the head of the bridge at the opposite end. It's an incentive for the exotic woman to cross over the bridge.

Callie: She sees the bus load of people. They are having fun and she wants to join them but she needs one more thing. (Callie adds the Indian figure.)

Paula: Who is he?

Callie: He's history; he's earthiness and kinda funny.

Paula: What happens when you put those pieces together with the bus load of people?

Callie: It looks like a party and she's ready to go over the bridge. (Callie places the exotic woman on the bridge.) Now she's in the middle of it all.

Paula: How does she feel now?

Callie: She feels great now. She's surrounded by good things, fun things, and pretty things She's off the island and is thrilled.

Paula: What are the good things Callie needs to surround herself with?

Callie: Humor, history, a few people. . . explorers of the mind, fellow writers and musicians. Having more humor in my life is the most important thing. I need to read more humorous works such as David Sedaris. I need to see humor in myself. I need to laugh at myself. I have been so driven and determined to finish my book my approach has become counter-productive.

Callie was writing a book on the history of the area where she lived until she encountered major writer's block. She tried to force herself to write but it was not working. She grew frustrated, became stressed and then angry. Everything in her life started to become meaningless as she grew more intense and determined to do everything in her life with serious conviction. . .including writing her book. This is when she started to drink excessively. It was a way of numbing the tension building in her body.

I suggested to Callie that she try some frivolous, nonsensical writing without depth or purposeful meaning to free herself up. I also encouraged her to write for herself without a goal or desired outcome. Callie's entire body language changed and a huge smile crossed her face. She had been feeling so frustrated and tense for so long she never entertained the idea that writing could be silly and non-goal oriented.

As a writer of historical novels Callie felt something was missing in the writing process. Her writing was weighing her down. Everything in her life had become far too serious and now this. Drinking helped her feel happy but it was short-lived. Whenever she drank too much—which had become far too frequent for her liking—the next day she would be extremely depressed and the joys that existed in her world no longer brought her fulfillment. Something had to change. . .life was too precious to Callie to waste being bogged down in an emotional funk. When the exotic woman eventually crossed over the bridge Callie said something huge shifted in her. She had now joined the others on the other side who were having fun and were free of tension. She responded with great enthusiasm to my suggestion to introduce herself to humor writing, and writing without an agenda.

Callie: That gives me such a great feeling inside. . .to write just for myself.

Paula: Allow it to be fun.

Callie: Surprise myself!

I ended the session presenting her with the idea. . ."What would happen if you played with your words in carefree, silly ways. . .what would happen if you talked to the cows?

Prince Charming

Gail was a wife and mother in her mid-thirties recovering from addiction. Her life had fallen apart. . .she was in the midst of a probable divorce, her three children were not allowed to live with her, and her health was quickly growing worse with each drug and alcohol abuse she inflicted on her body. One morning she woke up and realized she would likely be dead before the year's end if she did not make different choices. The addictions were destroying her body and soon her children would be motherless. She could not accept this as a possible future reality. . .she had to do something to change her destiny. She entered a program to help her create an addictive-free lifestyle. A Sand Play session with me was part of that program. She created her tray scene, went on a journey with her *knowing place*, and life for Gail altered forever when her soul spoke directly and honestly to her through her sand tray creation. This is an account of the highlights of her session.

First Impression of Her Sand Tray Scene

Gail: It looks like my story.

Paula: Did any feelings come up as you observed the world you created?

Gayle: Contentment and peace. . . .it's the first time in fifteen years I have felt this.

Paula: Was there anything in particular that evoked this feeling in you?

Gail: I see a transition. . . an important one. . .going from childhood into adulthood. It may seem odd, but I'm becoming an adult. I'm choosing to make different choices.

Paula: Is there a particular area in your tray scene you are most drawn to?

Gail: This area with the large rock in it.

Paula: What about this area captures your interest?

Gail: Several things. . .the corner contains my husband and myself. . .it's the real version, not the idealized version . . . and there is peace. We are standing by the rock and there's a cross on it. It feels built in and solid. There's a lamb and the sheep on the other side of the rock.

Paula: Seeing how this corner reflects back to you. . .what does it say?

Gail: Don't make idealized versions and then tear them down because reality doesn't match this version. . .accept them as they are. (Gail is referring to her perceptions of her husband and marriage.)

Paula: Does this change your view on how you'll deal with him?

Gail: I always saw him as Prince Charming, capable of doing and handling everything. In reality he's bleeding and in pain and was never allowed to show it.

Paula: Is this a recent discovery?

Gail: Yes, the reality hits strong seeing it in the sand tray. It's right there, so clear and obvious. My husband just told me the other day he doesn't want a divorce. The divorce idea was out of fear. . .he doesn't want me to die before his eyes. He's gathering strength to trust me one more time. As I view this area in the tray with my husband and me there is no doubt. I realize I have to give him permission to feel his fear. . .he's afraid. . .I never considered that. . .

Paula: Because of your idealized version?

Gail: Yes. He told his lawyer to not proceed with the divorce . . . he's courageous, which is more than I can say about myself.

Paula: Let's step back a minute. We discussed the idealized version and how you are now. . .that you are choosing to step out of the box to allow your husband to be real . . . a human with frailties. . .not the Prince Charming he has had to live up to. (As I say this Gail looks closer at the corner with her and her husband by the rock and realizes she too puts herself in an idealized version of who she thinks she should be.)

Gail: What I expect of my husband I expected from myself. It is unrealistic. . .beyond doing this, it's unfair to other people. He and I are both human with our frailties.

Paula: Who else was it unfair to?

Gail: Myself.

Paula: It's important to include yourself in the equation. It takes a courageous person of integrity to recognized this truth. . .to accept your humanness and frailties . . .to take your husband off the pedestal and allow him and you to be regular people. Now you are choosing again from a real and practical point of view.

Paula: I'm curious about Darth Vader*, the soldier, and sheep dog figures? (Darth Vader is a character from the Star Wars series, created by George Lucas.)

Gail: They are my children. I picked Darth Vader because my son is a "Star Wars" fan. The sheep dog represents my daughter. . .she loves big dogs. The war figure reminds me of my second son. . .he's crazy about soldiers. I also put the lighthouse in my scene to help me follow the light. . .the truth. Following the path from the light house is the path I must take.

Paula: What path is that?

Gail: It's not always smooth. Before I can get to the bridge from the light house, I have to face the beast. . .my addiction. . . represented by the tiger. The woman standing in front of the light house is me and the journey I have to take. I have to give up custody of my children and live apart from them and my husband for a while, until I recreate my life to include a non-addictive lifestyle. There are some things I need to come to grips with. Not being able to have more children, having to give up custody of my two sons and daughter, allowing myself and my husband space and time to heal and regroup from the traumas caused by my addictions. The clown, in my scene along with "Tinker Bell" (Gail is referring to a Disney character), represents childhood and when I developed my idealized ideas and fantasies. I have issues I need to address before I return to my family. I have no desire to repeat my addictive behaviors.

Paula: What is the biplane in your scene?

Gail: That's the adventurous part in me that's still alive.

Paula: What adventurous things would you like to do?

Gail: I'm going to start working again. I love to write and I want to find a job that involves strong writing skills. I want to teach aerobics again. . .that's at the top of my list. I want to return to Germany. . .I had a wonderful time touring there when I was seventeen. And I plan to take horse back riding lessons. As a child I loved horses.

Paula: I'm curious about the person carrying water?

Gail: This represents. . .not the guilt or shame she's carrying
. . .it's about earning back the trust of my family. It will
be an emotional hardship to be separated from my
husband and children. I have to be realistic about the
present situation, yet optimistic because I know I
CAN DO IT! I'm a strong-willed person. For years I
focused on the wrong things. . .but today I'm focused
on a realistic path rather than the idealized version.
(Gail then stated something that would make a
profound difference for her if she allowed herself to
bring it into full awareness.) "The illusion of the idealized life is not true happiness, it's a dream."

Paula: Bingo! You found out what is real and what is not, and
now you have the power of choice. . .to do what is right
and true for you.

Gail: My scene has shown and confirmed I am on the right
path. I'm traveling down the path leading from the
lighthouse and heading to the bridge. I will cross over
one day and return to my family. I no longer live in a
world of fantasy but a world far better.

After Gail did her session and completed her treatment she went
home back east. I heard within six months she was reunited with her
family and was doing well. She did go back to teaching aerobics and
landed a job using her writing skills.

The Plan and Approach
Has Just Changed

At the age of sixty John retired early from his thirty year employment with the government. He had made wise investments many years earlier in a company that has since become very successful. With retirement came some challenges. His long standing addiction to alcohol and beer had taken its toll on his health. A gifted and intelligent man, he was not sure what to do with himself. He spent a month in Sedona visiting from the east coast in hope of ending his addiction and healing his ailing health. Some professionals referred John to me for a session. After he completed his sand tray scene he shared his first impressions.

John: It's a Polynesian setting telling the story of the SS Bounty and its crew. "You are not a new man until you throw the old man into the well." It's a leaving home story. I'm not good at doing what people tell me to do. I always find a way around it.

Paula: If the SS Bounty story was your story who would you be and what would you do?

163

John: I'd be the Lieutenant who falls in love with the native girl.

Paula: How would you get what you want?

John: I'd get everyone on the boat to leave and then I'd take the girl.

John moves in a different direction with his story, not initially realizing he is moving into an area in his personal life that has caused him great challenge.

John: I would listen to the concerns of the crew, negotiate, then give them what they want and I'd get what I want. I'd stay quiet, so when I did talk people would listen. I know how to sit in a group so I won't get called to speak first. I wait until I can have the most effect. I have stories to tell, and I do certain things to create the story. I think three steps ahead. 1. I listen to the person. 2. I prepare a response but don't let anyone in on what it is until the time is right. 3. Then there is the measured response. I tell the person what they want to hear and I get the expected response.

Paula: What happens if the measured response doesn't give you the expected response?

John: It usually doesn't. (He discusses how he approaches his wife with the three steps to get what he wants and it doesn't work.)

Paula: So if the way you approach your wife usually doesn't work, why keep doing the 'three steps ahead' to get what you want? (John did not have a response. I saw he was uncomfortable with the question. It triggered a major life issue he had regarding his wife, he could not deal with just yet.)

Paula: Is the scene in the tray something you want for your self?

John: Yes, it is a two-year plan. I'll wait a long time for something I want. This scene is a place I'd like to go.

Paula: Where are you in the creation of your addictive-free lifestyle and desire to stop drinking permanently? (The psychologist who referred him to me wanted John to have a deeper awareness of who he was and the choices he was making in life.)

John: I can't drink again if I want to get what I want. I want happiness and health. If I drink I will get ill again and I will die. . .and so the decision is made. I choose not to drink because it interferes with my future plans and what I want.

Paula: This is your life statement. Where does your wife fit in?

John: She'll likely not stop drinking. Her family are all drunks. Hopefully, what I am doing will make an impression on her. I'll send her information on what I am doing to help myself heal and maybe her curious nature will make her read it. . .but I have to reinvent myself first . . .how she responds is her choice. . . if she likes what she sees maybe she'll want to stop drinking.

Paula: (I reframed what John said.) This is different than your initial plan to get what you want. You are focused on recreating yourself and letting others choose what they want to experience. It's their choice if they want to know who you are today.

John pondered the question, "Why would you do the three step plan if it does not work?" He had not avoided the question as I had thought. . .he had just been exploring an alternative solution.

John: I've been so obsessive about things but now I'm more relaxed and focused on how I want to do things for myself, and not make others do what I want them to do. If I focus on making others do what I want them to do, I'm not focused on what I want to do.

This was a real breakthrough for John. He saw that trying to manipulate others through his "three-step process" wasn't working. He decided to focus on what he wanted for himself, rather than trying to get others to do what he thought he wanted from them. THE PLAN AND APPROACH HAS JUST CHANGED.

John and I talked in person on a few occasions about his Sand Play experience during his stay in Sedona. After returning home he focused on his new passion—writing. He became a gifted writer during the next two years. It became the focus of his two year plan. I received a letter from him telling me I was on his list of the twenty people he felt had most loved and supported him. He died a few months later. Although his liver could not properly heal from the damage thirty years of drinking had done to it, his spirit had healed significantly and he was able to pursue the writing that had been a life's desire for the two year period before he died.

I Want Her Heart
Closer to Mine

Halley, age thirty-two, decided she wanted to surprise her husband Pat, thirty-six, with a weekend trip to Sedona to celebrate their fourth wedding anniversary. She learned about Sand Play work from my website and was intrigued. She called—and after we talked for a while—was convinced doing a couple's session would be a great anniversary present to give her husband. Halley scheduled a joint session. The couple arrived a month later.

Pat was one very surprised man when it first entered to studio. When he saw the sand tray, the expression on his face said, "What has my wife gotten me into?" Being a good sport he decided to go along after I briefly explained what we'd be doing. Before we even began the clearing process and setting the intent for the session Pat found himself drawn to particular figures, and he was hooked. . .and so was Halley. With curiosity written all over their faces, the couple joyfully created their joint sand tray scene and the Sand Play Soul Adventure began.

Immediately following the initial preparatory phase of the session and the creation of their joint world in the sand, I asked them for their first impressions as they communed with their scene. The smiles on their faces grew and their body language reflected that of two children eager to tell their story about playing in the "sand box of life."

Halley: The scene talks about our interests, memories and wisdoms.

Pat: Where we've been and wish to go. There's a lot of magic.

Paula: Do any feelings come up about your scene?

Pat: It reinforces we have a lot in common.

Halley: Everything Pat picked I liked.

Pat: There's lots of love. The hearts come together as one. (The couple had each placed two smaller hearts side by side next to a giant heart in their tray scene and had not initially realized they had done so.)

Paula: Are you surprised by this?

Pat: Not really but the degree of unison does. There's a harmonious flow throughout our entire scene.

Soon after creating their scene, each asked the other if a few of the items they had placed could be shifted around because something did not feel right.

Paula: How did it feel when you began moving each other's items?

Pat: It was fine. (Halley nodded in agreement.)

Pat: There's a lot of magical figures.

Paula: I noticed some items have been duplicated in your scene. Which ones are the most powerful for you?

Pat/Halley: Bridges, hearts, rocks, butterflies, trees and musical instruments. . .bridges and hearts are the most powerful.

Paula: Why are the bridges and hearts the most powerful?

Halley: "Past" is us coming over the bridge from different backgrounds. "Present" is crossing our bridges in life together now. "Future" is the future bridges yet to cross.

Pat: I felt similar. . .the crossing of bridges in our life is a team effort.

Halley: That's interesting. The bridges are placed in a circle.

Pat: They also feel grounding—linking us to the earth and in our lives.

Halley: They are also linking us to others. . .

Pat: Bridging our efforts together in reality. When we are in a magical place in our lives other magic comes forth.

Paula: What about the hearts?

Halley: Pat moved my heart.

Paula: Are you okay with that?

Halley: Yes, it's more exposed.

Paula: Why did you do that Pat?

Pat: I wanted her heart to be closer to me. (He looked at his wife with a tear in his eyes and she reached to hold his hand.) I placed the giant heart in an open position. It's not concealed.

Earlier Pat had selected a large ceramic heart and placed it in the center of the tray. On one side it had an opening. He turned it to that side as a way of keeping his heart open to Halley. Then he moved the heart she selected to be closer by his side.

Paula: What is the significance of rock energy in your tray scene?

Halley: We were married at Red Rock Crossing*. It represents our relationship, rock solid and foundational. (*Halley is referring to a beautiful scenic area in Sedona, Arizona.)

Paula: Pick up one of the rocks and just hold it in your hands. Let yourselves express whatever images and feelings come up as if the rock has a voice and can speak.

Pat: Returning to Sedona to the place we were married and standing upon the giant rock where we took our vows has recharged this rock and our relationship.

Halley: And it's recharged our individual energies. The rock in my hand has fourteen layers...meaningful experiences, memories. . .layers in a rock tells age, records history, tells a story. . .as in our relationship. These rocks in our hands are symbolic. It feels grounding and has depth and wisdom. . .

Pat: What has this rock seen? What does it take to round its edges? It's not perfectly smooth yet it has fine features like our relationship.

Paula: How do you feel Halley, when you hear Pat say that?

Halley: Hearts and strings. . .a harp playing beautiful music. (Halley's attention shifts to the figures of the Tiger and Jasmine from the Disney movie "Aladdin." Halley is glowing with a smile as she looks over at Pat.)

Halley: I picked "Jasmine" and the Tiger because on our first date we went to see "Aladdin." It directly connects to the rocks. . .the foundation of our relationship first began that that night.

We begin to explore the significance of butterflies—one of the duplicated items in the tray they said felt powerful, earlier in the session.

Halley: For me it's about transformation. . .metamorphosis for my husband. He loves butterflies.

Pat: Butterflies are so quick and they can travel so far. They can do much more than people think. . .like our marriage. It is far more than the outside world knows.

Halley: Our two ships are venturing out to various parts of the world yet at the same time are doing so in a circle. Our ships are coming in. We want to do a lot more travel-ing. We travel well together and easily meet people from other parts of the world and have more in common with them. I feel traveling is connected to our destiny somehow in a key way. We are destined to do something global.

Pat: We are about connecting with others in a global sense. I feel that strongly as well.

We talk about this in depth and explore how they can incorporate this desire into their lives. Halley is a successful artist and Pat is a financial planner at a bank. His job does not allow him much creativ-ity or freedom to grow in a global sense. Halley has more options to go global with her work. Pat wants to expand his horizons and cross over the bridge with Halley to directly link with others internationally in a creative and freeing way.

To assist them to tap into the *knowing place* of their soul I walk them through a visualization process. They enter a deeply relaxed state and I encourage them to step out of the present sand box scene and into the bigger 'sand box of life'. . .the world out here. I reframe what they shared with me a few minutes earlier as to how they see themselves taking their ideas and translating them through creative means in a global manner. I ask them to let their *knowing place* fill in the details.

Pat: One of my passions is writing songs. I can start writ-ing songs again for Halley to sing. She has an amazing voice. It's been a long time since I did this for her.

Halley: We can also do joint explorations together. . .maybe couples' retreats in exotic places. Pat has the business background and I have the connections. . .and we both have participated in numerous self-discovery and personal growth seminars, and workshops as a couple. We have lots of wonderful information to share.

They continue to receive information from this place of heightened awareness. It is clear that, as a couple, they are well matched and operate as a harmonious, happy team. Each are very much individuals, respectful of each other's differing ways, yet in sync with what they want to accomplish in life as a couple. It also became obvious both were ready to take their relationship to another level. I felt an intuitive nudge to ask them about their music.

Paula: Have you ever performed together in public?

Pat: The last time was ten years ago shortly after we first met. We loved performing together. Halley sang so beautifully it brought tears to many people in the audience.

Halley sheds a few tears as she goes back in memory and talks about that experience.

The session went over an extra half hour at their request. We could have easily continued for another two hours. I wrapped up the session by summarizing what they had said and made a few additional suggestions.

Paula: Connecting with others on a global scale is a strong urge within both of you. Your individual energies want to expand and be shared globally as a couple Doing so in a creative capacity while sharing your talents and skills through performing together, facilitating couple's retreats, or even inspirational speaking as a couple are important pieces to consider integrating in your growing relationship. I strongly encourage you to explore these possibilities in more depth. Give them a voice. Take short trips, like you are now, on a regular basis. Perform together again for family and friends, perhaps even in a local venue. . .a coffee house perhaps. Start brainstorming for a couple's retreat . . .get the energy moving. You are both ready to take your relationship to the next level. There are many possibilities to explore.

Pat and Halley left in an elated mood. I met them a few months later and we had dinner in Phoenix. They were both in a good place with each other and their marriage. Halley started to perform again and Pat wrote songs whenever time permitted. Halley had just renovated her website to include the international market to sell her art and her husband helped her reorganize the business portion to promote her art work. They were brainstorming on how to combine their love of travel with their interest in working with couples in an inspirational and creative setting.

I Want to Come Home

Adrian was a young lady in her mid-twenties referred to me by Reverend Marion. My colleague had been working with her for several months and felt her client would benefit from a Sand Play session. Adrian's one session proved insightful. It offered her the necessary pieces to take crucial next steps in her healing process. She had been sexually abused as a child and Marion felt the young woman was ready to face and deal with beliefs she made long ago as a result of the abuse. The choices she made were presently causing major problems in her life.

Adrian entered the studio feeling uncertain—yet willing to try a Sand Play session. Trust was a huge issue for her as she did not know me. Sensing this, I assured her we would not do anything that would make her uncomfortable. If at any point she wanted to stop the session that would be all right. I briefly explained what we'd be doing, did a clearing ritual, set the intent, and then she collected the miniatures for the scene. As she created her tray scene there was an air of determined strength and resolve that the next step in her healing would be revealed. She quickly relaxed into the process. Her *knowing place* seemed to be right by her side helping walk her through the session.

> Adrian: I need something red. My scene is still not done. (She adds a red bird.) I need something pink. (She picks a rose quartz crystal. . .and decides at the last minute to get a rock, trees, and a rat, putting these items in her scene.) Now it's done.

> Paula: What is your first impression of the world you created?

> Adrian: All the things I put in my scene represent my life and how I feel about things. They explain how I view things. . .past, present, future. I needed items with specific colors for my personality. The red represents love, the pink crystal is where I want my energy to go . . .I want to be a healer.

> Paula: What are you most drawn to in your tray? (She selects a green glass ball approximately eight inches in circumference. We explore the significance of this item in her scene.)

> Adrian: It's clear. . .it reminds me of breath.

> Paula: Take a moment to breathe in that clearness of breath. Allow yourself to feel its clarity. Let this energy embrace every cell of your body. (Adrian moves into deeper relaxation and is present and receptive to direction.)

> Paula: Allow that clarity to speak. What does it say?

Adrian: Help!

Paula: Help with what?

Adrian: (Adrian is drawn to the rat and horse in her scene.) The horse is a foal, and the rat is my addiction. . .what I use to cover up and hide.

There is a house in the center of her tray. The rat is on one side of the house and the horse on the other.

Paula: What is the house about?

Adrian: This is a place I feel safe.

Paula: Allow this safe energy to embrace every cell of your body. When you feel fully connected to that safety tell me about it. What does the safe place want you to know?

Adrian: It's about fun and magic, believing in life, love, God, feeling safe. . .knowing everything is going to be okay . . .everything feels right.

Paula: Do you have a safe place to go to in your daily world?

Adrian: I visualize angels. . .and do affirmations to keep my thoughts positive.

Commentary: To help Adrian anchor her safe place in concrete form, I suggest that when she returns home she write about her safe place and what that looks like in daily life. I also encourage her to draw it since she likes drawing. Combining the visual with the story would help anchor her safe place in physical form. When she does not feel safe and needs something tangible, viewing her picture and reading her story will remind her that her angels are present and available, if she should ever forget their support during times of fear and upset. Adrian felt this idea would help her remember when fear tries to make her feel unsafe.

I also suggest that Adrian take relaxing baths with nice smelling bath salts or oils on a regular basis to help her feel nurtured. I recommend she allow images she equates with safety such as angels, or the color red for love, to help her safe place come forth and speak to her during times of challenge and distress while in a relaxed and meditative state—perhaps while she is relaxing in the bath. Afterwards she could write down or draw a visual of what she experienced, heard and saw. This would be a time for her to allow the clarity and wisdom to share its knowing. . .from her safe place.

Paula: I'm curious about the necklace in front of your house.

Adrian: It's Native American. It is earth-centered and spiritual. It runs through me and touches everything in my life. It's a natural expression of "Mother Earth."

Paula: Does this energy make you feel safe?

Adrian: Very much so.

I continue to focus on the energy of safety, knowing that feeling safe is a rare experience for a person with a history of being sexually molested as a child. Doing activities that make a person feel safe is an important piece in the healing process. When Adrian talks about the necklace, her body language and tone of voice clearly indicate she is drawn to the nurturing and centering qualities of the natural earth.

> Paula: I suggest you spend time communing with nature . . .hiking, sitting by water, reading books in which nature speaks through story, for example, "Talking with Nature" by Michael Roads.

> Adrian: (Adrian points out a white rabbit in her scene.) I don't know why I picked him. Bunny rabbits are safe. . .they have the ability to be. . .

Adrian starts to intellectualize. I have found that at this point in the session it is important for the person to stay with the feelings they are experiencing. It is common for adults who were sexually abused as children to avoid being in their bodies in a feeling sense. They tend to disassociate and disconnect from their emotional bodies. In many instances it was a safety mechanism that helped them to psychologically survive the abuse as children.

> Paula: If it is comfortable for you, take the bunny rabbit and put her to your heart. Allow yourself to feel her wisdom. . .what does she say?

> Adrian: I feel a childlike energy. . .it says I grew up too fast.

> Paula: Why was she sitting by herself in the scene looking away from everyone else? Is she isolating herself?

> Adrian: Yes. . .within me a piece of her broke off and separated.

> Paula: Is it to do with her innocence?

Adrian: Yes.

At this point Adrian's voice grows quiet. Her body language is showing, "Please be gentle and walk me through this very carefully. I could easily crumble." I reassure her again that we will only go as far in the process as she feels comfortable. She nods and says she is doing okay and wants to continue.

Paula: What does the bunny rabbit want you to know? (Adrian begins to cry.)

Paula: (Intuitively I'm guided to ask her the following.) Does she want to come home?

Adrian: Yes. She's scared. Home was a place she thought of as safe and she was violated.

(Adrian speaks in third person, unable to relay her experience in first person.)

Paula: When Adrian takes care of what she needs, does it become safe inside to be her?

Adrian: Yes.

Paula: So whenever you are taking care of yourself it is safe for her to come home.

Adrian: That home is safe. The other home was not and she does not want to ever go back there.

Paula: She does not have to go back. Her safe place is with you if you take care of yourself.

Adrian: She's beginning to believe that. . .and she will believe it more so when I take better care of myself on a continual basis. When things are right inside me and she feels safe she comes out—like now. She loves the little glass bottle in my tray. It contains magic, youth and excitement. . .all the things I thought were lost to me. . .I can see and feel these are still present in me.

Adrian has begun to mix first person and third person as she speaks. She smiles and becomes childlike in her mannerisms—in a playful way—but is still very much the adult.

Adrian: I really like my tray and I want to climb the rock over there. I can feel the power of the rock. . .it feels strong and it makes me feel strong when I stand on it. That rock is intellect. My favorite glass bottle with the magic, youth and excitement in it wants to spill out all over my tray scene.

For Adrian, the energy of the bottle and the rock is a nice balance between her mind, emotions and body. The rock has a grounding quality for her as do the other items from the natural kingdoms of "Mother Earth." When she opens her bottle it is important she feels safe, centered and grounded. I show her the book "Everybody Needs a Rock" by Byrd Baylor and suggest that she read it.

Adrian: I feel so relaxed. At the beginning of the session I was feeling nervous and upset. I didn't know what to expect.

Paula: What changed?

Adrian: I'm looking at the big picture of my life. . .I can see it in my tray scene. (Adrian turns the bunny rabbit around so she can see the scene.)

Adrian: She no longer feels a need to isolate herself. She wants to be part of the scene. The red bird is looking at the child and feels lots of love for the child. The horse I moved to the corner is my present self. I'm still feeling my emotional wounds from the sexual abuse. . .and I am still child-like in how I handle my life; however, there's lots of room to grow. The castle on the hill is solid and safe. The crystal in the back of the castle reminds me of something I saw in a vision when I was thirteen. I saw myself as a healer. I didn't understand then but I do now. I can help other females who have been through what I have. I am a survivor. Whenever big changes are about to happen I dream of water. I dreamt of an ocean last night. I never thought I could feel so good and empowered playing in the sand. I love my scene. It gives me hope and strength that I will one day be a healer, and that I will heal all my emotional wounds.

Adrian left the studio smiling. Later that day, with her approval, I filled Marion in on what happened during her session. Marion said she had seen Adrian soon after I did and that her client was glowing and felt the most optimistic about her future that Marion had ever seen.

Ron and the Minion

One afternoon I received a call from a mother regarding her son Ron, age ten. She had heard about my work from a number of parents and felt I was the right person to work with her son. She told me that a week before, Ron said he was going to get a shotgun and shoot his father. (The boy's parent's were not married and no longer lived together.) After thinking long and hard, however, as to whether this was the best option to take, Ron made a different choice. He decided that if he did kill his father he would have to go to prison for a long time, and that would not make the pain or fear he felt inside go away. It would make it worse. Instead he had decided the best course of action would be to kill himself and then he would not ever have to feel the horrible feelings that continually haunted him ever again. His mother wanted to act fast and got him to see me as soon as possible. Ron promised his mom he'd meet with me before doing anything drastic. . .but he didn't feel it would make any difference. In Ron's mind, his problems with his dad would never go away. Killing himself was the only answer.

When I first met this boy he was feeling hopeless, depressed and very angry. His eyes lit up the first time he walked into the studio and saw all the miniatures on the shelves with a large sand tray in the center of the room. With little instruction it was clear to him what came next. Ron went to the shelves and picked several warrior-type figures, including some dragons, created his tray scene and went to battle. It was he and all the warriors who wanted to destroy and see him dead. Heading the team of attackers was the Minion. He said this was his father.

Ron came back a number of times and his battle scene went on for several weeks. As the weeks went by Ron told me his story about his relationship with dad. In his mind he felt his dad would soon annihilate him. Yet the more he played in the sand tray, the stronger Ron became in mind, body and spirit. The pain and fear he felt being with his dad was released into the sand tray scenes he created. His mother told me Ron really enjoyed coming to the studio and thought I was cool. I listened to his stories and watched him do continuous battle with the Minion. Each time Ron went to war he added a few more warriors to fight for his side. No matter how many warriors joined in to defeat the Minion, this destroyer would come back from the dead to terrorize and kill Ron in the sand tray. His visits with his father continued to send Ron into ever deeper states of rage and depression. The Minion was always the victor and there was no hope of survival for its victims, especially the Minion's son.

Ron's mother was legally required to allow the dad to visit him. She had no physical proof of anything going on behind closed doors and Ron refused to tell the courts what was happening. He said, "If I tell, my dad will kill me." The only two people he would talk to were his mother and me. At one point he created a scene in which he was buried at the bottom under a huge pile of sand. On top of the mound was a massed heap of warriors with the Minion standing victorious on top. When Ron was told by his father that he would be spending summer vacation with him it nearly sent Ron over the edge. I was truly afraid Ron would follow through on his threat of suicide.

I had a session with Ron in which I asked him if he would consider speaking to the Judge and telling him why he wanted to kill himself. He agreed to tell the Judge how he felt because if he was forced to spend the summer with his dad Ron said he would kill himself. With the help of a paralegal, his mother, and me, the courts were informed of Ron's intentions and an emergency session was held. The Judge did not want to speak with Ron—he wanted to speak with me. An interview by phone was scheduled. I spoke with Ron, and he and his mother gave me permission to fully speak on Ron's behalf. I spoke to the Judge through the eyes of Ron. I did not accuse or judge the father's behavior. I had never met the dad or seen him with Ron. I could only testify as to what was going on in the boy's mind. I told the Judge I was not willing to take the chance that this boy might kill himself. The sand tray scenes he created, the stories he told me, and how he was behaving during his sessions left no doubt in my mind that if Ron was forced to see his father, especially for the whole summer, it would send him over the edge, and he would probably kill himself. I urged the Judge to listen to the boy's plea. . .and he did. The father was denied visitation with his son for a six-month period. That is when the true healing began for both father and son.

During this six-month period, doing the sand tray work and playing a variety of therapeutic games, a normal ten year old boy emerged. He started to smile, laugh, be obnoxious, and play with friends more (when he was with his dad he was not allowed to play with friends) and he was no longer afraid the world would be destroyed by aliens. It came out that Ron's father had some strong beliefs about extraterres-trials and told stories that terrified Ron. During this six-month period the boy became a totally different person. He discovered who he was without his father's controlling influences. . .and the best part was this: the father decided to make some healthier choices in order to have a relationship with his son.

His father sought counseling, took parenting classes and slowly grew to realize that his behavior, in large part, was alienating his son and that something needed to change. It was a rough six months for this man, yet he made the changes and after that time period had passed, the Judge granted the father visitation with his son. . .which was only to happen in the secure environment of his counselor's office.

Ron was terrified to go into counseling with his dad and started displaying some of his prior behaviors. He had not seen his Dad in six months and did not know the counselor. The depression and fear returned tenfold. He could not trust things had really changed. . ."My dad will never change. He will pretend to be different and then he will begin to do strange things again."

It took several weeks for Ron to see that his father was becoming a different person. Over time Ron became stronger and surer of himself, physically, mentally and emotionally. He knew he felt differ-ent on the inside in a good way; however, he still questioned his dad's intention. Fortunately, in time, step-by-step, the sand tray work and the "giant blue ball" worked its magic.

Ron and I would hit a giant blue exercise ball back and forth in the studio sometimes for the entire session. You would be surprised how many creative and ingenious ways a ball of this size can be hit...and how often my miniatures ended up in all sorts of creative places on the floor whenever we lost control of the ball. I have never laughed so hard with a client as I did with Ron. With wall to wall shelves filled with miniatures there were plenty of opportunities for a major disaster to ensue but it never came. . .and miraculously nothing in the studio ever broke.

Ron began to feel tiny sparks of hope just knowing his mother and I stood by him no matter what, and he finally he realized his dad was taking measures to change. I must give credit to his father. This man had significant emotional/mental problems according to the psychological assessment ordered by the courts, yet he did everything in his power to make things right between him and his son. Not being allowed to see the boy was a major wake-up call for him, and if he wanted to have an ongoing relationship with his son, there would have to be a dramatic shift in his parenting style. In the meantime, Ron grew in strength to a point that he stood up to his father and spoke his truth. When he didn't like something his father was doing he let him know. The tables had turned and Ron was in the driver's seat. It took almost two years for Ron to reach this point. He came to me when he was ten and by the time he turned twelve, my involvement and support were no longer needed.

Ron has since made his peace and co-exists with his father in a way that seems to work for them both. They now have fun together, and the dad has learned to lighten up and enjoy life more. I know his mom and dad are happy their boy decided in favor of life. Ron fought his ultimate battle in the sand tray. In the last series of sand tray scenes he created he was no longer defeated by the Minion, and the battle scenes took on a quality of playful fun, natural for a twelve year-old. Ron has become his own person, with his own voice, and is now a force to reckon with.

The family has since moved to the West Coast. The last I heard, each parent lives in a different town a few hours drive apart by car. Ron has an ongoing relationship with both parents as he travels back and forth between households.

I'm Okay, I'm Strong, and I Am BACK!

Don was a corporate lawyer in his forties from Texas who, for the most part, loved his job until he hit a few snags climbing the corporate ladder in the law firm he worked. His work became a source of great stress and frustration, and he did not know why. . .he only knew something was missing. In the meantime his way of dealing with these emotions was to drink alcohol in large quantities. This was easy since going out for drinks with clients was a common occurrence. A few extra drinks would go unnoticed, or so he thought. After a few years of increased drinking, his family, his body, and health did notice. Don realized something was seriously amiss when he started making significant mistakes on the cases he was working.

Because he held a high value on quality health and well-being, Don sought help to stop his drinking before it caused irreparable damage to himself, his family and career. I was one of his stop off points in his process of healing. Don wanted substance and meaning in his life, and to be happy. His career was no longer providing it. The sand tray scene he created provided a crucial key, and what he discovered utterly surprised him. It was so simple, yet potent. He and the sand box became instant comrades on the journey back to health and wholeness.

Don's First Impression of His Sand Tray Scene

Don: Looking at my creation from where I sit, I feel some anxiety. I just placed things anywhere and didn't feel like there was a purpose. However, when I walked around my scene I felt better. I looked at it from different angles and it began to make sense. It gave me a broader perspective. . .from the bigger picture.

Paula: What do you see?

Don: It feels like my life story. I feel like I am coming full circle. It feels good. . .a sense of completion is near. I'm beginning again. I'm the cyclist in the scene biking home after a long, rough day at the office. I look forward to going home. The cyclist is reflecting on his day and realizes everything happens for a reason.

Don and I discuss some of the realizations he's making about his life and the choices he made in the last few years. He said a part of him was shut down in the process of working toward his career goals. He'd take on huge cases and do all the work, not asking for help from others. Don comments. . .

Don: It is tough trying to do everything myself. . .it doesn't work.

Paula: What does work?

Don: Listening to my inner self. . .it is very clear in my tray scene. I like the giant heart I placed in the center. It makes sense. It helps me be aware of what matters— how I do my life and where I do it from. (He cries softly.) It's about accepting all of me – who I am in the big picture. When I work a case I look at all the angles to make sure I've covered all the groundwork so the entire story can be revealed. I don't want any unpleasant surprises. This approach usually works well for my cases. I have not allowed the same consideration for me. It's all about love. I stopped letting love into my life as I became too task-oriented.

Paula: Where do you go from here?

Don: "This above all: to thine own self be true." I've traveled a long way in life. My heart...that's the answer. Over here is my innocence. (He points to a figure that represents his youth.)

Paula: What does he say?

Don: I've broken through and I'm heading home. I am okay, I am strong and I AM BACK! It's what is. It's the truth. . .as long as I remember who I am.

Paula: What has Don the professional decided?

Don: "The thinking Don" has decided to take a rest and let the heart take over. The cross perched on the heart tells me victory is at hand. . .I must maintain a balance between heart and mind. Do some pro bono work just for the pleasure and satisfaction of helping someone else, knowing that justice has been served and some-one's life was improved as a result.

Paula: Who's that on the hill in your scene?

Don: He's my meditating monkey. I picked him because he looked comical yet serene. He makes me smile. He's telling me? "I TOLD YOU SO!"

Paula: What did he tell you?

Don: "Happiness is an inside job!" He's on the highest hill in the tray. He sees the over-view of everything going on in my scene. He sees from the bigger picture of life.

Paula: What about the stop sign?

Don: It's reminding me to stop hiding from myself.

Paula: (Summarizing and reframing what Don has said.) When you view your world from a place of balance between your heart and mind, you can see the whole picture. This allows you to have a clear view of what is going on . . .much like the cases you work on. Victory is there for the taking. Remember what the meditating monkey said, "Happiness is an inside job." Going home to your inner self and living from the big picture of who you are is also an inside job. The choice is yours to make.

Don left smiling, content and at peace having found the "something" missing in his life. The last I heard he was doing well in his career, personal life, and living an addictive-free life.

The Tiger and the Devil

Chad was a man in his thirties who worked as an administrator. When he first walked into my studio we had no idea what was about to unfold or that the journey we were about to embark on would shake his inner world to the core and free him from a reality of which horror movies are made. He came to see me once every two weeks for eighteen months, and then a year after that two separate times, three months apart, to check in and work through a few lingering issues.

The challenge that brought him to me was his inability to sleep properly during the night. Chad suffered from horrific nightmares and restless sleep. Functioning during the daytime became nearly impossible. He said he felt like a 'walking zombie' during the day, barely able to do his daily tasks, and yet he somehow managed to function, be in a marriage, and be gainfully employed. He had been going to a psychologist for a few months; however, talking about his challenges with sleep did not resolve the problem. The psychologist, having heard about the success I was having with clients utilizing the tool of Sand Play, as a way of unlocking hidden fears, suggested he see me.

The doctor knew that whatever was causing his client's nightmares was not likely to expose itself through talk therapy.

The first time I saw Chad he made an elaborate tray scene—placing a lot of figures representing powerful images that made him feel strong and able to deal with whatever might come his way. Although he could not remember his nightmares, he knew whatever was causing them was dangerous to his health and well being. It felt as if his life was on the line and that he could be destroyed in a blink of an eye.

While creating his very first tray scene, something magical and empowering within his being felt present, ready and willing to come to his assistance. He only had to ask and they were there for him. After this session, Chad said he felt hopeful for the first time in many years. He felt would be able to discover the source of his nightmares. And maybe in doing so, he could take back control of his life and have a restful sleep.

Over the next several months, one figure was present in a number of his scenes. . .a fierce looking tiger significantly larger than most of the other miniatures. This was Chad's power animal he felt the most connected with during his Sand Play. The other power figures also served to strengthen his fragile self. Then one day, a few months after we began working together, Chad said he was having flashbacks from childhood and he was feeling very afraid.

During the process of setting the intent at the start of Chad's sessions, he would call in his "power figures" to assist him through this challenging time, especially the Tiger and Shaman. They became the focal point of the facilitation. Slowly, step by step, we worked with each flashback that surfaced. On many occasions Chad's body became stiff and it was clear he was entering a state of terror; however, he did not want to stop the explorations. Whatever was going on, he wanted to know, and to find a way to deal with it. He no longer wanted to be a victim at the mercy of some unknown fear. He was also frequently guided to put the Wolf, Wiseman, and the Sun and Eagle Kachinas (from Hopi Lore), along with the Tiger and Shaman, into his tray scenes. He felt they had the wisdom, strength and knowledge to help him conquer "the unknown" he described as evil and wanting to destroy him. The cartoon characters of Gumby and Pokey (known for their rubber bodies and flexible postures) also often surfaced in his creations. They taught Chad how to bounce back quickly and easily from one of his terrifying episodes triggered by this energy he felt was evil in intent. With each tray scene he created and processed, he grew stronger mentally and emotionally. He felt the time was nearing to allow his dreams to come to life in the tray. As long as his support team, especially the Shaman and Tiger, were present he felt ready.

After working with Chad over several sessions to anchor these power images in his psyche, there was no doubt that a divine and loving power was guiding me on how to facilitate and utilize visualization to help him tap into his own divine source. Whatever was about to be revealed, it was huge and scary for Chad, and it was buried somewhere in childhood memories. After approximately six months the flashbacks shaped the story of what happened to him as a child. . .and resulted in nightmares during adulthood, too frightening to remember.

It is a courageous and amazing journey Chad went on in order to survive. His willingness to face the memories of horrendous childhood abuse, and choosing to no longer be a victim of an unspeakable cruelty, is what is truly remarkable and deserving to be told.

When Chad was a child his parents were members of a Satanic Cult that practiced ritualistic sacrifice to honor the Devil. He witnessed inhumane acts of violence, and holding the weapon doing the deed, was one he knew as the Devil. When Chad grew older he realized it was a person dressed in a Devil's costume. . .however buried deep within his childhood mind it was the Devil himself.

After the buried memories fully surfaced, the Devil figure in Chad's dreams threatened to kill him or worse. For the six months following this revelation of what had happened to him as a boy, our sessions focused on helping Chad find the courage to face the Devil so he would no longer be afraid. . .Tiger energy was the key. One day, a year after I first started working with Chad, he entered the studio a changed man and said: "Paula, the Devil came to me last night and it felt so real. He was angrier and scarier than on previous visitations and he wanted to annihilate me. Next thing I knew my Tiger came into the scene. He was fierce and powerful. He looked at the Devil, walked over to him and said, 'Your reign of terror has come to an end!' He ripped the Devil into shreds and it was done."

For six more months, Chad was not convinced it was over. On a few occasions the Devil entered his dream, however, when it approached him, he looked directly at the Devil and said, "Sorry, it's not going to work, you no longer scare me."

I asked Chad where the Tiger was when this was happening.

He said, "The tiger is me and so is the Shaman, Wiseman, Wolf, the Sun and Eagle Kachinas, and all the others who support me to be in my own power."

I knew at this point our work together in the sand tray was completed. Chad was sleeping much better—at least six hours on most days—and the Devil could no longer terrorize him. It would be a few more months before Chad felt safe and secure enough, within his own power, to not require my services. One day Chad stopped calling for sessions.

A year later he asked to come and see me. This time it was due to major stresses at work. The second time had to do with his wife Lilly whom I mentioned earlier in the book. When Chad is in a vulnerable place the Devil sometimes returns in his dreams, trying to convince him he's unworthy and deserves to be destroyed. Once he calls in his power team, particular the Tiger, the empowered Chad takes over and soon he's in control of how he is responding to the stress. Inevitably, as his inner reality shifts so does his outer world. Once he resolves his issues, the Devil vanishes and his sleeping patterns return to normal. The last time Chad was in touch with me he was doing well and was very much in control of his destiny.

Differences Make the Heart Grow Fonder

Reverend Marion referred Cole and Indy for individual Sand Play sessions and then a couple's Sand Play session. Their sessions were to be part of their seven-day intensive with her. These are the highlights of the couple's session I facilitated.

Cole and Indy's First Impressions of Their Scene

Cole: One corner has a magical air about it with its castle and wizard...the back of the sand tray feels linear and false, too much in a line, too constricting, too compressing . . .the adventure corner is interesting with the binoculars in it. It leads out of the sand tray...there's no place of rest in the scene where it's not too busy...right now it looks like a playground with lots of fun things to do.

Indy agreed with Cole that the scene was too busy and chaotic. Cole felt reassured by Indy's observation and both quickly realized this was reflective of what was going on in their daily life.

Indy: The river in the middle makes a diversion for me...one side feels fake and old. Cole picked a lot of plastic things, I prefer the natural. Where I put the bench and tree is a place of rest. The adventure corner leads the way to something bigger. I do not have to stay in one place. That part feels comfortable. I did not like the mechanical vehicles Cole picked.

Cole: (Cole is not offended by Indy's remark.) Where the tree and bench is. . .the place of rest. . .I would like to expand it.

Indy: I agree!

Paula: You may expand the "rest place" if you wish.

The interaction between Indy and Cole was strong and pro-active. Very little facilitation was required. I allowed them to go with their own organic flow and did not intercede. Their thoughts, feelings and wishes expressed to one other were heard and respected by each other. Cole and Indy have very different temperaments, however, the mutual acceptance and respect for each other's differences was deep and abiding. This was made clear by the shifts that took place in them through the changes they made in the tray scene. It happened quickly and easily and was beautiful to watch.

They removed a large portion of the linear objects and a lot of the extra items that had surrounded the resting place to give it more space for peace and quiet. Cole added a house near the quiet, restful place to show that it was close to their home. Indy smiled in agreement. She created a gateway to the castle and said, "The castle is a starting point from which all the magic in life is given an expression out into our world."

The couple energetically worked together to create a mutually agreeable and harmonious scene throughout the entire session. Each explained to the other why they felt something needed to be changed in their scene. They tried the changes to see how they both felt before making a final decision whether to make the change permanent or not. It was a true team effort.

Then the process of changing and adjusting took on a quality of seriousness. Cole wanted the fun portion of the scene to balance the seriousness. Indy chose to widen the river to allow more flow between the two worlds. Cole added Pinocchio and a wooden car and placed the puppet into the car for fun. Indy added some musical instruments in the fun corner for creativity. Before they made these changes each asked permission of the other if it was okay to do so. This went on for another fifteen minutes. Both Indy and Cole thoroughly enjoyed recreating their tray scene to match what their hearts desired as a unified couple.

Indy: It feels more balanced and safe now.

Cole: It feels more peaceful, ordered and purposeful.

Indy/Cole: It feels more natural and in harmony with who we really are and where we're going in our marriage.

Cole: It has a mix of the serious, fun, restful, magical and adventure. . .and the freedom to move in between worlds making the scene more balanced.

Indy: In the original tray scene we created I wanted to leave the area...now I want to stay and be part of the adventure.

Cole: It's not just all fun anymore, it has everything in it and there is space to rest and just be. (Indy agrees)

Paula: Look through the binoculars at your world. What do you see now?

Commentary: Earlier in the session the binoculars played a prominent role in their scene. The quality of having adventure in their lives was a crucial piece to renewing their desire to be with each other. Before the intensive with Marion their marriage had been in trouble. Their lives were chaotic, busy and void of curiosity and adventure. They felt their relationship was in jeopardy and did not know if it would survive. When they looked more closely at what they created together in their sand tray scene both were amazed and surprised that the love and bond they share is still very much alive in themselves and their marriage. Viewing their scene through the binoculars helped them focus and bring home the reality of who they truly are in relationship to each other, themselves and their marriage.

Indy: Where are the figures that represent us in the scene?

Cole: We are everywhere in the tray. The castle, the trees, Pinocchio, the musical instruments, the binoculars . . .we are the magical expression of the experience we created for ourselves in the tray scene. This is who we are together when we take the time and space to create what our hearts desire. (Indy smiled in full agreement with her husband's final observations.)

Paula: You allowed and surrendered at your point of mutual agreement, neither had to give up anything. You let go of your attachment to specific results and allowed the bond of love and respect for each other to lead the way.

The Boss' Chair

Loni was visiting Sedona for a much needed rest and to take time out from her family. She had been experiencing challenging health problems, and though she could function in her daily life, her life did not feel like her own. Too often she felt at the mercy of her varying ailments. She had had enough and wanted to take back control of her life. She went on a five-day customized healing retreat, and was scheduled to see me for a sand tray session by the person who had organized her Sedona journey.

As soon as Loni entered my studio she was instantly drawn to the therapeutic game called "Life Stories". . .even before she selected miniatures for her sand tray scene. This was the first time something like this had happened with a client. There was an air of mystery and intrigue surrounding the session even before we began the facilitation. I did the customary clearing and set the intent for her session. Before creating her scene, Loni selected from the Life Stories Game one card from each section out of a possible sixty cards. As a result of this action, something of great significance was about to take place. We began the journey by exploring Loni's first impressions of her tray scene.

Loni: It's evoking images of long ago. I'm feeling a lot of frustration and emotional pain. "The Boss Chair" in the left corner is a future strength to be awakened in me.

Paula: As if it's already awakened, allow that place of strength to speak. What does it say?

Loni: I need to be the Boss of my life, my thoughts, my feelings and desires. . .I need to rule my life.

Paula: In what way does the Boss want you to rule your life?

Loni: Decisions about my future need to come from my innermost feelings.

Paula: Allow the Boss to move you into your innermost feelings place. What would she like you to know about you from this place of awareness?

Loni: There are many parts to me. I'm an Empress/Amazon-like woman, an adventurer, explorer. I'm a great mother, nurturer, giver. I'm also a princess/goddess, and a pioneer woman. I'm a young maiden, a fairy princess —full of life, play and fun. I am all those things seated in the chair called the boss. . .and she's in charge. She's clearly rooted and seated in this chair and regulates and orchestrates everything in this world. Once I'm in charge, it's a whole different ball game.

I asked Loni to state three times with full conviction, "Once I am in charge it's a whole different ball game."

Commentary: Often when clients receive a message that dramatically shifts their energy physically, mentally and emotionally, and makes them feel empowered (as it did with Loni) I encourage them to use it as their own personal affirmation. Since it is drawn directly from the individuals' own words, it is often more self-empowering and helps them move into a more centered, positive and balanced place. I suggest they create time and space to anchor the affirmation by stating it least three times with strength and conviction. In the process of doing this, I recommend clients inhale and exhale full relaxing breaths from the heart and solar plexus region. Breathing this way can help them energetically feel the power behind these words and serves to empower their mind, body and spirit. In Loni's case, after doing this, she experienced a dramatic shift in how she thought and felt, becoming more pro-active in her healing journey during her session.

Loni shifted the items in her scene differently from how they were first arranged with focused determination. She semi-buried a giant shark that was once prominent in her tray. . .moved the ceramic heart to the corner she described as her place of strength. . .buried the alien three quarters of the way into the sand. . .took the deep sea diver and stabbed the shark, then held the giant heart to her own heart and hugged it along with the plush dog. On the ledge of the tray she placed a baby doll that was previously buried in the sand.

Paula: Wow, you have taken charge. How does it feel?

Loni: I love knowing I have the power to shift my reality. It's all up to me. I don't have to be at the mercy of unsavory and destructive forces.

Paula: You are absolutely right.

At this point I gave a homework assignment to Loni, as I often do with clients after they experience a breakthrough. I specifically encouraged her to do activities in her daily life that empower her to claim her strength and take charge of her life. . .as powerfully as she had done in the sand tray.

We then explore what it feels like for her to say, "Once I'm in charge it's a whole different ball game. I'm the boss." As she does this I encourage her to let it be fun and playful, in a "fairy princess kind of way", so she can feel a sense of joy and happiness being in this person- ally empowered place. Loni spontaneously picks one of the four cards she had previously chosen from Life Stories board game, and reads it.

Loni: "Describe something that made my father happy." It made my father happy to buy me toys.

Paula: Why do you think you picked this?

Loni: To remember that fatherly love I lost long ago. I need to remember the support and strength of father energy that once existed and has since been forgotten.

Paula: Where do you want to go next in your scene? (Loni picked "Green Slimer," a ghost character from the movie "Ghostbusters.")

Loni: This green blob figure is a part of me that jumps in and trips me up. . .it tries to tell me I'm not good enough. It's the insecure self who lacks belief in me.

Paula: What does he need to help shift this way of thinking?

Loni: He needs "who Loni is" when she sits firmly in the boss' chair. He needs a firm hand from my place of inner strength.

Loni took Green Slimer from his prominent place in the tray and placed him in a subservient position.

Loni: He's still there but he's not in charge. It's all about balance.

Paula: Is it time to read another card?

Loni: Yes! It says, "What is something satisfying about work?" I'd answer, "Having fun and playing."

Paula: I suggest that you introduce an element of fun and playfulness into your work life. As a university professor, in charge of developing and teaching your own classes is this doable? (She nodded in agreement.)

Loni: My heart's desire is what will bring me self-fulfillment and earning power, as will the act of giving to myself and others.

We explored a figure slumped on a couch placed by himself in the tray.

Loni: It's me. . .I have a long relationship with emotional and physical weakness.

Paula: What does he need to feel stronger in these areas?

Loni: To not allow illness to rule my world.

Paula: Call in the support of your heart, your innocence, your children, the plush dog and anyone or anything else in your tray scene you feel empowered you. Ask these expressions or parts of you to help work with your ill parts.

Loni took all the figures representing sadness in her world and put them in the heap of things to be discarded. She also added the bride carrying the husband, representing the old ways of being in her marriage, to the heap along with the shark and deep sea divers. I'm intuitively prompted to ask Loni what she does when her children are sad.

Loni: I hug them, rock them, and help them understand the sadness can be dealt with through Love and then I help them tune into their strength.

Paula: What's missing with regard to when you're sad?

Loni: I have to be as good to myself as I am to my children.

Paula: So then taking all the sadness in your tray scene and putting it on the heap to be discarded, is that an ideal thing for you to do?

Loni: No, it's not the loving thing to do. I would never tell my children to discard their feelings. I encourage them to express them while I hold them in my arms and just love them.

I reminded Loni how she shifted her energy, quickly and easily earlier, by going to her place of inner strength, and knowing within. She took the heart figure and plush dog, embraced them, and became strengthened as a result. This placed her in the empowered position of "The Boss."

> Paula: Loni, this is a crucial piece for you. Honoring, nurturing and loving yourself as you do your children is equally important.

Loni added two figures to her scene, the fairy princess and a figure she called "the realized total woman" and stood them next to an item she referred to as her "higher spiritual self." Loni read another a card from the Life Stories board game.

> Loni: "Tell about one of the happy traditions in your family." My father loved to sing in the church choir.

> Paula: Allowing good positive memories to enter your thoughts seems to be the reoccurring theme with these cards. Allowing the whole story to have a voice and not just the painful memories, is another important consideration to make when reviewing your life.

Loni nodded yes, then she talked about the remaining miniatures in her tray scene.

Loni: The ship is me still floating on the water, however, I'm headed to shore – my ultimate destination. I'm no longer lost at sea. The wolf is the independent me . . .the restless me. . .but he's a noble and adventurous figure with a lot of powerful strong attributes...he's a beacon of light for the ship when it, "I", gets lost.

Loni read the last card she had selected from "Life Stories" game. We looked at each other in awe of the synchronicity of her picking this card.

Loni: "Tell a story about getting lost and finding you way back home."

Several months later I heard from the lady who organized Loni's healing retreat that Loni's health significantly improved and she was much happier in her career. Also, she and her father developed a closer relationship with each other. Loni had moved into "The Boss's Chair."

How to Do Sand Play
for the Soul

- Part V -

And a man said, Speak to us of Self Knowledge,
And he answered, saying,
Your hearts know in silence
the secrets of the days and nights,
But your ears thirst for the sound of
your heart's knowledge.
You would know in words that which you
have always known in thought.
You would touch with your fingers
the naked body of your dreams.
And it is well you should.
The hidden well-spring of your soul must
needs rise and run murmuring to the sea;
And the treasure of your infinite depths would
be revealed to your eyes.
But let there be no scales to weigh your
unknown treasure;
And seek not the depths of your knowledge with
staff or sounding line.
For the self is a sea boundless and measureless...

The Prophet
-Kahlil Gibran-

"Just say, 'Yes, I want to know who I am so that I may walk in life with my head held high, my arms spread in surrender, and my heart wide open to all that is good, loving and wondrous. . .'"

- Paula Petrovic, the Sand Play Lady -

Doing Sand Play for the Soul

The main requirement for participating in a *Sand Play for the Soul* experience is to show up and be present. You are embarking on a journey that begins with you, and you are the sole creator of what comes next. This section offers you guidelines and suggestions on to how to venture forth. There is no right or wrong, only moment to moment creation.

The first step is allowing yourself to start with a clean slate. Like that of a new born baby, when life was just beginning and the story not yet written. Being present, willing and available to dialogue with your *knowing place* through moment-to-moment surrender is where it all begins.

Next is choosing a setting in which you feel safe to do a Sand Play experience, or modified version, and having your tools at hand to begin the process. The exploration may begin once the key pieces are in place: the sand tray or other sacred holding space; some miniatures and treasured belongings available for easy use; and you being present, willing, and able to embark on this journey.

Are You Ready, Able and Willing to Do Sand Play?

Before you even begin your Sand Play Adventure, check in with yourself to learn whether you are ready, able and willing to begin this journey with a clean slate. Below is a visualization and exploration to help determine how prepared you are to do Sand Play.

Visualization for Sand Play Readiness

For ease and convenience have someone you trust, whose voice is soothing to you, to read this section out loud or make a recording, allowing you the freedom to participate in the visualization.

Sit upright in a comfortable position. Close your eyes and allow your mind, body, and spirit to move into a place of quiet surrender. Take deep, relaxing breaths to ease you into a state of calm serenity. Breathe in restful, calming, free-flowing air. Exhale tension and mind clutter. This is your well-earned moment to release all of the demands and stresses of your day. Allow yourself to fully enter a state of peace, ease and surrender.

When you feel ready, visualize with eyes still closed, as if you were opening your eyes for the very first time. The first thing you see before you is a tray-like container filled with a soft, cool sparklingly substance. It urges you to touch it and feel its textured substance. Soon your curious nature engages you and you begin to look around your environment. To your delight you see all sorts of shapes and forms that invigorate and awaken your senses. What you see makes you feel alive and wonderful inside.

The first desire you have is to take some of those appealing shapes and forms and put them in the tray of textured substance situated before you. As you do this, your attention and focus is so drawn to the task at hand that nothing else exists except the wonderful aliveness you feel inside. As you continue this action something grabs your attention, taking you by surprise. You discover it is you and your actions making you feel this wondrous sensation. The textured substance, shapes and forms are stimulating to your senses; however, the real excitement is you participating—and that is what is making you feel so good and so alive. It is YOU, making it happen by simply allowing it.

Now allow yourself to come back to the here and now. Ask yourself: Do I experience a thought or feeling inside of me that says something to the effect, "Yes, this experience feels good. I want more"? If you do, and you want to feel even more of this positive feeling, I encourage you to proceed. Answering this question in a positive way means you are willing and open to doing Sand Play. However, if fear, discomfort and resistance surface during this visualization then I recommend you do not continue at this time.

Note: Doing a Sand Play experience for yourself, as outlined in this book, must be an activity that feels good and right for you to do. It is meant to be an uplifting, insightful and a fun opportunity in which to tap into your own knowing—an aware sense within that recognizes what will help awaken the best in you. It is essential that you feel safe and comfortable during the journey.

Being healthy, happy and successful is something you must claim for yourself. The key to creating what you desire is to imagine it, feel it, and allow it into creation. Focused intent is far more powerful than just telling yourself you want it. You have to authentically want and be willing to go for it! Remember: being only partially committed to what you truly want denies you full access to what can be. The process of creating what you want in life, and being fully committed to it, begins with YOU! "It's an inside job."

Two key components to successfully doing the Sand Play process are 1) A willingness to open yourself to the possibility that there is more to you than you may realize, and 2) the desire to tap into that expanded version of you. Whether or not you have these two components can make a significant difference in how a Sand Play journey is experienced.

> The Soul will never force, intimidate or manipulate you into doing something you are not ready to participate in. *Sand Play for the Soul* is gentle, nurturing, and user friendly. Anything that does not feel nurturing, empowering and safe is not "*Sand Play for the Soul.*"

Cautionary Note: If you are in a fragile emotional, mental, or physical state, my first recommendation is to seek out an experienced and trained professional skilled in the area of your health concern, who you feel safe with and who can assist you in your healing process. Sometimes all we need is a helping hand when our life challenges become too big and overwhelming to handle on our own. Many people come to my studio troubled or disturbed by a life upset or challenge in their lives and leave with smiles of hope and resolve. It has been my experience that asking the right questions and receiving the right support can go a long way in helping us successfully resolve problems.

If, after reading this book, you feel *Sand Play for the Soul* sounds like an experience you'd like to try, and it feels right to embark on this journey of discovery and realization, then that's your cue to take it to the next step: Create the setting, gather your tools and do Sand Play!

Just remember. . .being present and attentive to what is right for YOU in any situation is a crucial piece to a healthy, wholesome, healing process.

Sand Play is about discovering more fully who we are in the larger picture of our lives. Unhealthy and destructive choices are made by people every day, mainly because they do not take the time to make informed decsions. Lack of information, hasty judgments and fear of what is not understood can cause harm, heartache and devastation. If we had the "know how" and self-confidence to draw upon our own inner resources we would have a better chance of resolving our problems with greater ease and success. Through Sand Play you can learn how to tap into your own innate abilities to successfully address and deal with those issues that prevent you from living a healthy, happy, fulfilling life.

Sand Play is about discovering more fully who we are in the larger picture of our lives.

Too often we are told and shown what is wrong with us and not what is right. As a result, we tend to be masters at negative self-talk. When the "negativity disease" invades our mental, emotional and physical bodies it surfaces and often acts itself out in harmful and unpleasant ways. An old saying rings true to me. "We can do nine things right and one thing wrong and what are we likely to focus on?" I have frequently witnessed with clients, friends and in the general population that the mistake we make receives much more of our attention than the accumulation our successes.

One of the greatest joys of sand tray play is that when you look upon a creation you have made, **you get to see the "best of you" actualized into three dimensional form and discover what is right within you and well in your life. You have the opportunity to see the wise, strong and aware person who is able to do what needs to be done to solve your problems.** The focus is on what is successfully working within you and in your life to help correct what is not working.

Opening Clear Communications with Your Knowing Self

Four central areas of action are necessary to assure open and clear communications with your knowing self.

1. Begin with a clean slate.

2. Be willing, ready and able to do the work.

3. Attend to the logistics of doing Sand Play, or an Alternative Approach

4. Do a clearing, set the intent, create your sand tray scene. . .and have fun with the facilitation process.

1. Begin with a Clean Slate

It is true we have made mistakes and wished we could have done things differently. It is also true that who we are today is not who we were when we came into this world as newborns. In the moments following our birth, our personal stories were yet to be written. Almost immediately, opportunities to grow and learn became a way of life for us as children. We were introduced to the positive and negative aspects of human living. Influences from parents, siblings, close relatives, teachers, peers, cultural and societal values, spiritual or religious affiliations and the media all impacted our lives in innumerable and varying ways, on many levels of daily functioning

When Life Turns a Negative Page it's Time to Clean the Slate

When negative emotion enters our lives, judgment and condemnation towards self or others have a habit of wreaking havoc and disarray. Fear, pain, hurt, grief, rage and so many other emotions can have a devastating effect on our lives. When we allow forgiveness and compassion to become prominent in the ocean of our human emotions, we see quite a different story. Profound revelation and miraculous recovery finds a home for expression. Some of the most moving stories I have observed were born out of those clients who chose to embrace these highly revered qualities. Forgiveness and compassion are empowering emotions and have tremendous capacity to heal and transform lives at a deep level. It is these qualities which are most needed in times of upheaval, yet too often they seem to elude us. This is when starting over and making choices in favor of life is crucial.

There is no greater enemy than we who are an enemy to ourselves. When destructive action has been inflicted, the resulting shock can trigger a negative reflex emotion, provoking greater upheaval and trauma. The greatest sadness in human history is what we do to ourselves and thus others. The saying, "Do unto to others as you would have done unto to you," can be tricky if what you do to yourself is condemning, hurtful and destructive. However, there is a way out. . .

The sand tray offers an outlet to diffuse the enemy within and to awaken the friend instead. The story of Lilly "Where did the Fear Go?", introduced earlier in this book, is a wonderful example of what can happen when the wise and healthy knowing parts of a person's psyche are given voice and expression. For Lilly, fear and terror no longer held her captive. A more empowered, self-knowing Lilly took charge and the fearful Lilly faded into the background losing influence over her.

> *The sand tray offers an outlet to diffuse the enemy within and to awaken the friend instead.*

When we allow ourselves to operate from a full deck of cards, with all our resources at hand to play the game, the opportunity for success increases many fold.

Life's Sad Story Turns into Hope as We Choose Again

Wouldn't it be terrific to access a place of clarity and knowing that tells us the whole story and not just a partial version; the one that includes the good in us capable of performing great acts of kindness and accomplishment, and not just those parts of ourselves deemed unhealthy and harmful—so that when we do choose again we can use our strengths and wisdoms to make healthier, more informed decisions?

Doing *Sand Play for the Soul* allows us to look at our story from a receptive and accepting place, not a judging place. The best and knowing parts can show how to recreate your life in a way that complements what is good and right for you. Your soul does not focus on your weaknesses and short comings—what is wrong with you! It focuses on your strengths, abilities, and what is right about you!

Allowing yourself to begin with a clean slate—you and an empty tray filled with sand, free from past history and future expectations like that of a new born—is the first step to doing *Sand Play for the Soul*. For this journey to bring you positive, empowering, life-transforming benefits you must first begin anew. It's just you, the tray, and a brand new opportunity to go on a journey of self-discovery and realization.

2. Willing, Ready and Able to Do the Work

Before determining what will serve in your highest and best good, you must have a reference point to establish what is true and right for you. Something in you must say, "Hmm, that's interesting! There's something here I want to explore. Let's give it a go, shall we?" If the willingness to try something new is present, off you go on this new adventure. If you're not willing, there's no point to continuing. It would be like blowing bubbles in the pouring rain. Nothing would come of it except empty motion.

Perhaps you find doing Sand Play is not quite for you. . .that's okay. Just reading this book and hearing other people's stories may be all that's needed to motivate you to consciously dialogue with your *knowing place*. You may discover other pathways to self-discovery that can open you to your higher knowing. I invite you to read "Alternative Approaches to Doing Sand Play" in the latter part of this section.

Side Note: During times I've facilitated people in a sand tray who were going through a challenging time, my assistance became necessary to help them walk through and beyond the trauma in order for them to reach a place of breakthrough and transformation. It is important to pay attention to your limitations and what is needed to take proper care of yourself. You may be ready and willing to explore Sand Play and yet you may not feel able to facilitate your own journey. This process can be powerful and revealing.

One man, in his early fifties, a Harvard graduate and financial planner who worked on Wall Street for many years, came to my studio for a session. As he walked through the door, he unexpectedly found himself in-stantly drawn to a wooden dollhouse. As soon as he saw it

Our sand tray creations provide us additional and useful information to help us make informed, healthier decisions.

he broke into tears. It became apparent he had entered another time and place. He told me, "I have not cried in years. When I saw this house it reminded of a house I lived in with my mother when I was three years old. It was a painful time for me. I totally forgot about it until now." I helped him walk through this flashback. In one double session, as information surfaced during his Sand Play, he released a life insecurity that made him distrust himself and his abilities every time he had an opportunity to be part of a large money-making venture. His fear, previous to this release, had caused such stress that he experienced extreme burn out and prematurely left a profession he dearly loved. After this experience, he opened a consulting firm in his area of expertise and did well both personally and professionally.

For the sincere seeker, Sand Play is a tremendous tool for self-exploration, discovery and healing. However, should doors to memories and emotional wounds suddenly and unexpectedly open-up, causing you emotional, mental or physical upset, please take a deep breath, exhale, and turn to the section called, "Sand Play Safe Guards." For a person who has been through serious trauma, and has not had the benefits of appropriate, skilled, therapeutic assistance to help deal with the trauma, Sand Play needs to be seen in a more serious context. Doing this self-facilitation process is not advised. Please seek professional help.

Sand Play for the Soul is intended to be fun, insightful and reflective of where we are in our lives. Our sand tray creations provide us additional and useful information to help us make informed, healthier decisions, especially if we are fully open, willing and receptive to what this exploration process can offer—such as in the case of an artist who was facing a major life decision. When he came to my studio he was fully ready and willing to find out what his soul had to say about what was really going on. Here is his story...

This successful artist, a man in his late forties, came to do a Sand Play because he was concerned his restless and unstable moods were adversely affecting his family. The man was entering a major crossroad in his life and marriage. He felt his family was at risk of disintegrating and his behavior was largely responsible.

Fred loved his family dearly and wanted to understand what was keeping him from making healthier choices regarding these relationships. When he came to me he was open, willing and receptive to doing the experience and be fully present throughout the entire facilitation. His attitude significantly and directly affected what was about to unfold. Within the first ten minutes he had placed a miniature of a birthday cake in the center of his scene. During the facilitation process, we explored the significance of this item. Within minutes he broke down crying.

Similar to the financial planner, Fred reverted to a time around the age of three. A devastating event happened during his third birthday in an exchange between him and his parents. The initial unhealthy dynamics between them carried throughout Fred's childhood until the present. In this release of emotion, triggered by placing of the birthday cake in the center of his scene, Fred began to understand the strained dynamics of his challenging family situation.

Fred realized he was operating at half throttle. To uphold his parent's values and expectations, he denied a crucial part of himself full and natural expression—his intuitive and creative abilities. As a result, he had become a frustrated artist with difficulty completing his commissions on time. This frustration carried over into his dealings with his wife and children. When Fred realized what he was doing and how his attitude and behavior negatively affected them, he wanted no part of it. Through his sand tray creation, he made a deep inner decision to not hold back as an artist, and not to live by the constricting values his parents had instilled. Because Fred was ready, willing and able to hear what his soul had to say to him in the sand tray, he was able to receive the information he needed to hear, loud and clear.

In the following months Fred took the necessary steps to heal unhealthy family ties. He became less frustrated and more productive as an artist. He allowed his soul to communicate more readily through his creative endeavors. Fred became a much happier person living a life that reflects who he is and not what others thought he should be.

3. Logistics of Doing Sand Play: The Setting

Where you set up your tray when you do Sand Play can be just about anywhere, just as long as the space selected feels physically safe and comfortable, and you can freely move around your sand tray to look at it from all sides. You do not have to have a studio or special room to do the work. I've traveled outside my studio to many different settings with my portable sand tray and mini-collection. Hospitals, hotel rooms, schools, homes, and even a Kung Fu Dojo, have been home to Sand Play sessions.

The key to doing Sand Play successfully for personal use is to create a sacred space in a setting in which you and your soul can dialogue with each other without outside distractions or interference. Once you have created your sacred space, next is gathering tools necessary to give three-dimensional form to the dialogue between you and your soul. These tools, and how to use them, are in the sections that follow.

The Sand Tray

Before you is an empty tray of sand. The size and material of the sand tray varies according to your needs and desires. It is made of wood, plastic, or almost any other safe material. I do not recommend glass. (If the container cracks or splinters for any reason glass fragments could mix with the sand.)

Ideally, the size of the tray accommodates your full peripheral vision, if your eyes were looking directly at the tray's center. The reason is that the ease of seeing your sand tray scene fully and clearly without having to make an effort helps maintain your focus. You need to do nothing but see directly what is there right in front of you. That said, however, if you are guided to have a larger tray you can. It may not be practical for moving the tray around manually, yet if you really feel you need a larger tray go for it. It just means the experience you have may change, and that's okay. You can always add a smaller version later.

The tray's interior is painted blue, symbolically representing the sky and water. Water, sky, and sand (representing the solid earth) make up the core of the physical world we live in. The sand can come from just about anywhere, and be any texture and color.

When I went for my certification in Sand Play Therapy, my instructor had trays filled with white, black, red and purple sand. It sure added a different perspective and quality to the scenes. If you have a favorite color or texture of sand you prefer, by all means use it. Mini Zen garden trays have recently become more popular. The designs one can make in the sand with the tools provided have brought peaceful serenity to many.

There are few restrictions to the type of sand one can use. I would, however, recommend heavier textured sand. If the sand is too powdery, it gets very messy. It is also wise to make sure the sand you use in your tray is clean, especially if collected directly from a beach. I got my sand from Lake Powel, Arizona. Living in Arizona where the sun gets toasty hot, I took the sand I collected and naturally baked it for a few hours in my back yard under the sun's purifying rays. I turned the sand over, stirred it, and let it bake in the sun for another few hours. Sun baking is a natural way to air out and disinfect the sand.

You can also bake the sand in the oven. Placing sand to the rim on a cookie sheet and baking at 300F for fifteen to thirty minutes should do the deed. Also, take note that today many beaches tend to be polluted. Depending on where you get your sand I also suggest washing the sand two or three times in liquid detergent before baking it—

whether naturally under the sun or in your oven. The easiest way, but not necessarily the most fun, is to buy sand in a store, such as a building supply store. Make sure sand bought in a store is clean and play-safe for children, and guaranteed hygienic and safe for human touch.

How often you clean the sand in your tray depends on how often you use it, and whether you had clean hands while creating your sand tray scene. I work with clients on an ongoing basis so I purify my sand more regularly than you might. Children who come to my studio with dirty hands are asked to wash them before doing their tray scenes. If you are especially sensitive to germs you will want to purify the sand more frequently.

****

Now the sand play vehicle is complete with sand, sky, water and earth and is ready for the creation process to begin. Whatever shall you put into this world? What you put in your tray scene is almost unlimited, as long as it is small enough to fit in the tray and does not move on its own. I strongly recommend you do not put live creatures in your sand tray scene.

One of the greatest gifts the sand tray brings to the exchange between the Soul and Self is: we of the physical world who like to see, feel, touch and experience our reality through the concrete versus the abstract can do just that. However, since the Soul is not specific to the tangible world, often mystical, magical, and ethereal elements of the unseen world may be present. Sometimes unusual activities or experiences can occur. If they do, embrace them as part of your journey and open yourself to discover what the experience has to offer.

Sand Play and Objects of Significance:
My Personal Collection

Over the years facilitating Sand Play, I have gathered a vast variety of miniatures. The journey first began with the figures I bought from Valerie, the Waldorf teacher I mentioned earlier in the book. Then I sorted through my own personal knick knacks, including those bought during my world travels, and added them to the collection. Next came items from the animal, plant, human, mythical and spiritual kingdoms. I gathered natural items from the earth herself, went to stores, yard sales, and received gifts from clients and friends who felt their treasured possessions needed to be in my studio collection.

Within the first two years the core of my collection was complete. Over the next several years the gathering of miniatures continued. Currently, I have thousands of miniatures, representing many aspects of the three-dimensional world in which we live. Rocks, trees, plants, animals, shells, water creatures, people, buildings, household items, land vehicles, ships, airplanes, mystical, spiritual and religious figures, musical instruments, cartoon characters, extraterrestrials and other imaginary creatures, toys of every description. . .and the list goes on. Items ranging in size from a fraction of an inch to a few feet tall (though most are six inches or less) have found a home on my shelves. They are present in my studio for anyone to use in their Sand Play creations. No figures are insignificant and they do not need to look a certain way. They come in all shapes and sizes.

Special Treasures

You may find some unusual and unique objects. By all means, include them in your collection if they speak to you. I'll share some of my special treasures:

One is a double heart hand-made by a young girl, gifted to me as a Valentine's present. Another is a beautifully hand-painted wooden egg from another girl thanking me for letting her play in my studio. This child had challenging behavioral problems. The dad, who raised her as a single parent since she was a toddler, was at a loss what to do and brought her to me. At age six she wanted to leave one of her treasures with me. She is now a young adult, and her highly creative and unruly energy has found its way into an acting career she is pursuing full throttle. Her father says that at eighteen she still vividly remembers the Sand Play sessions and workshops she attended. Another of my personal favorites is the rock collection given to me by Sung, the Tibetan boy I spoke of early in the book.

Then there is a prized chess set of hand-crafted ceramic figures, renditions of characters from JR Tolkien's book, *The Hobbit*, a client had commissioned for her private collection. She came for a Sand Play session to work on upsetting life challenges. During the facilitation she felt the "energy of Christ" give her an important message. She came to a valuable realization that assisted her through trying times. She sold me the chess set to support my work. One character from this chess set, Gollum, is especially popular. People who select this figure do not always know him as Gollum. With large, green, translucent eyes, he evokes deep emotions and wisdom in participants who use him in their sand tray creations.

One man who chose this figure to put in his sand tray creation was *Si-Gung Paul Szasz, a Shoalin Kung Fu Master and Priest. During facilitation, Paul experienced a connection to a universal knowing, the "Place of Oneness" central to the Buddhist's philosophy, in a way he

---

*Si-Gung Paul Szasz owns and operates Golden Tiger School of Kung Fu in Kitchener, Ontario, Canada.

had not before. As a Buddhist, communing with this *knowing place* was a normal part of his daily practice. Professionally, his dojo with many students did well; however, his personal life was strained. For some time he felt separate from this state of "Oneness." Exploring the figure with the green translucent eyes, Paul reconnected with the serene, transcending peace. Experiencing his *knowing place* to the degree he did that day was empowering. The disconnection in his personal life dissolved, inner peace returned, and Paul re-awakened and re-integrated "Oneness," eluding him. He gave credit to the symbolic significance of this figure and the facilitation. The rest of his tray scene also revealed vital information.

Your Personal Collection

In your own house you may discover treasures of every variety that you can use to begin your collection. They may be buried in boxes, dresser drawers, or closets. There may be goodies on your shelves, counter tops, tables or under the bed. . .or they can surface in the form of knick knacks, figurines, statues, jewelry, framed photos, and toys from your childhood or your own children (if they are willing to share them). All these can mark the beginnings of your personal collection. Party places, craft shops, hobby train shops and toy stores are great and inexpensive places to buy miniature trees, flowers, houses, people, animals, cartoon characters, and household items . . .anything and everything imaginable that exists in our three dimensional world can find a home in your Sand Play collection.

Specialty gift shops will have religious, spiritual, mythical and historical figures. Swap meets and yard sales are especially delightful places to discover your figures. Some of my most unique and interesting pieces come from these places. Collecting your miniatures can be an exceptionally, enjoyable adventure.

The items you select for your collection should reflect as many spheres in your world as possible: people, physical structures, items from daily living, earth and animal kingdoms along with representations from religious and spiritual realms that are significant to you. The really special treasures can be hand made gifts or presents gifted to you by a loved one.

After you form your initial core collection, be sure you have quick and easy access to it when it comes time to do a sand tray scene. Having your core collection and personal treasures within reasonable distance when you create your scene is the most ideal. It is best if you do not have to spend long periods of time searching for items to put in your scene. The focus needs to be on the creation your scene. It is okay if you have to go to other rooms for a few specialty pieces as long as the process of collecting them is not a lengthy one. Again the attention is intended to be on the actual creation of a scene.

Summary: Areas of Action 1, 2, 3

The key to Sand Play success for personal use is to create a sacred space in which you and your soul can dialogue with each other without outside distractions or interference. The sand tray, or sacred holding place you use to put your treasures or miniatures of significance to you, can be in a variety of settings. All that is required is a safe, comfortable and private place; the tools to give form to the Soul dialogue—your personal collection within easy reach for use; the willingness to begin with a clean slate and be present, ready and able to participate with what unfolds.

Important Note—Recording Your Session: Before you begin have something at hand to record the information you receive during your journey; a piece of paper, note pad or journal along with your pen, pencil, color markers or other writing or drawing instruments. If you are not keen on writing information down, you can use a tape recorder. If these methods of recording do not work for you, you may have someone else witness your journey and write down any information that comes forth. One caution: have another person record for you ONLY if this person can be an impartial observer and is someone you completely trust. In essence, they would be similar to a court recorder. The person records ONLY what you say. This person does NOT interact with you during your Sand Play journey. Facilitating journeys with another will be covered in the upcoming sequel. *Sand Play for the Soul: A More in Depth Look.*

4. The Clearing, Setting Your Intent, and Creating Your Tray Scene

Before you begin creating your tray scene, clear yourself of mind clutter and set the intent for what you wish to accomplish in the session. State your intent clearly, concisely and briefly.

Setting the Internal Stage to Do Our Soul Creations

1. Situate yourself in a relaxing, safe, distraction-free environment. Position your body to be comfortable. Sit close to your sand tray space where you will do your soul creation.

2. Clear your mind of busy thoughts and mind clutter to the greatest extent possible. The clearer and more present you are in the moment, the freer and more able you will be to let your soul speak through your creation. Breathe from the abdomen and allow your entire body to be fed with this wonderful, life-sustaining, nourishing air. Continue breathing deep, calming, breaths while releasing old air and tension from your body.

3. State your intent. The format I use is simple, concise and brief. Too many words clutter the mind and sidetrack us. You want to give your mind and body greater access to the *knowing place* through a clearly stated intent.

Clearing the Mind and Setting the Intent

Take a deep, relaxing, full breath. With each exhale fully release all the events and thoughts from your day and allow yourself to move into a neutral space. Do this releasing process at least three times, more if needed to come to a place where you are calm and relaxed. When you feel you are in that neutral space, ask the *knowing place*, "the place that has all the answers," one question: "What do I most need to know about my life at this time? Show me the way."

At this point, you are not seeking a specific response. You are only setting the intent for the session, anchoring the question so that the *knowing place* becomes consciously activated. Keep breathing full relaxing breaths while exhaling tension from your body. When you feel ready, begin spontaneously selecting the miniatures for your sand tray scene. As you choose the pieces and create your scene, stay conscious of your intent. This assists you to maintain your focus during the creation process.

While creating your tray scene HAVE FUN! After all, you ARE playing in a sandbox! You are the sole creator of your world. Anything your heart desires is for you to choose and place in your world.

Facilitating Dialogue with the Knowing Place of Your Soul

Before you begin creating your sand tray scene with your gathered items and doing the self-facilitation, make sure your means of recording the session is readily available. After you follow the self-facilitation process covered in the next section, and its time to begin exploring the significance of your scene, record the information that spontaneously surfaces though your thoughts and feelings; however, do not focus on what you are writing at this time. Later you may go back and review the details of what you recorded. Recording is useful to gaining greater insight and understanding about your session.

Important Note: If a lot of activity and energy stirs in your brain when you ask the suggested questions listed in the "Self Facilitation" section, please STOP. You are probably thinking too much. The intellect serves a useful purpose in our lives; however, other aspects of human expression, such as the heart, body, spirit and emotions also offer vital information. If your thinking mind is analyzing and processing—as only the intellect can—immediately shift your focus to the region of your heart. Take a few deep breaths and release the busy mind activity with each exhale until you feel your mind quiet down, allowing your heart and body to join your experience. The only thought you should have is what is happening in this instant—here and now! Allow your *knowing place* to share its expression with you through your sand tray scene. Your soul awaits and desires nothing more than to speak with you through your creation. Focus your energy in your heart. When you allow your heart to speak, and not your head, you are ready to begin the self-facilitation. Just remember: if you are feeling tension, busyness, or activity in your brain, shift attention to the area of your heart. Take a full relaxing breath from the abdomen; fill your body with fresh, life-sustaining oxygen and exhale. Release all the "thinking" mind stuff. Let yourself experience a huge sigh of release, even sigh out loud if you need. . ."Get it out of you"—to make way for your heart and soul to have its voice.

The Self-Facilitation

Take a quiet, peaceful moment to observe the world you have created. Allow whatever, thoughts, feelings and impressions that spontaneously arise to quietly come to the surface of your conscious mind. You are communing with your creation and allowing it to affect you with its knowing. Now walk around the tray. Observe the world you created from different angles. Does any information change as you view your creation from different perspectives? At this time you may add, take away, or shift any miniatures in your scene. Once you have walked around your tray and have come full circle, you will begin the facilitation.

First Impressions: When you first observed the world you created did any thought, feelings, or impressions come to the surface? If so, what? Maybe the total scene, or only a portion caught your attention. Perhaps one specific miniature stood out. Any and everything that captured your attention, no matter how minimal or major, is significant. DO NOT JUDGE THE THOUGHTS. Write down or record whatever comes up for you. What you are doing is a form of free association. If you are thinking about the impressions received, STOP, take a breath and move your consciousness into your heart area.

Note: First impressions are not about analysis. They are simply pure initial feedback. The *knowing place* is clear, concise awareness of WHAT IS, in the moment—before preconceived ideas, judgments, personal beliefs and past history step in to influence what we think we know. In this place we are re-connecting to something untouched, untainted, all-sustaining, coming from The Divine. Here it all makes sense and has purpose and meaning beyond the constriction of limiting beliefs. . .here we are free. That which is Divinely-driven has the resources to make all things possible. How we receive this is what comes forth during the facilitation determines the outcome.

Facilitation Questions

Once your creation has introduced itself, through your first impressions, jot down any thoughts, feelings and impressions that you receive. Next is the journey itself. Step-by-step you explore in greater depth the significance and meaning of each miniature or cluster of miniatures in your scene. The following questions are offered to help you facilitate a deeper discovery of what your soul wishes to reveal to you about your life at this time.

1. What area of your sand tray or miniature(s) are you most drawn to at this time? Take a moment to experience your attraction to this item or cluster of items.

Write down whatever spontaneously comes to you. As you do this, if a specific thought or emotion is triggered make note of it. In essence, you are dialoguing with the symbolic representations of the miniatures in your scene, as if they had a voice of their own. These entities, as expressions in your sand tray, are a means by which your *knowing place* helps you open communication channels. Your tray scene is an extension of you: The best and knowing part of you through which your soul speaks. Asking effective questions holds the key.

Asking Effective Questions: How do we know if we are asking effective questions? Often, this is a result of personal interpretation. The thinking, logical, analytical mind is a tricky phenomenon in the human experience—it can convince us of almost anything – even if reality or the truth is far from what the mind is telling us. And, of course TRUTH is subject to interpretation.

The first and most important component to successfully asking an effective question is to keep it simple. Be specific. Ask exactly what you want to know. Use this as a guideline:

- How do I feel inside when I ask this question?

- Does it feel like this question gets to the heart and soul of the matter?

- Does the question help me discern what's really going on?

- Can I get the information I need to get on with my life as I want to live it?

The more clear and concise questions we ask, the more informed we become. When we are dialoguing with our chosen figures in the sand tray the principles are the same.

For example: You are drawn to a particular miniature in the tray and as you look at it more closely a sense of great joy surfaces from within. Ask: What about this figure makes me feel so joyous inside? Does it remind me of someone or something in my life that has had a similar impact on me? If so, who, and in what way?

Some questions may prompt you to ask another question in a similar vein. Write down whatever spontaneous impressions come to you. Or perhaps instead, you were attracted to a particular cluster of figures and they impressed on you a sense of sadness. You feel so sad that you begin to cry. After you acknowledge that sadness what might you want to know about it? A natural question could be, "Why do I feel so sad when I look at this group of figures? Does one specific miniature make me sadder than the others? If so, why? How does it relate to the others? Is there a connection? Allow the answer to surface from your heart, not your head. When the answer comes, write it down. The answer that spontaneously comes forth may surprise you.

It is important to listen to the response without judgment. Simply write down the information revealed and, when you are ready, move to your next moment of experience. If something significant and revealing is offered during this process, spend a few moments with the realization. Let yourself experience it from the heart, mind and body. From there, if another question arises, flow with it. Let it help you hear what your scene wants you to know. Remember, the intent has been established. . .you asked your *knowing place*, "What do I need to know about my life at this time? Show me the way." When you stay in the moment, in the Now and connected to your heart, asking the right questions becomes easy.*

Once the question is asked, the answer will follow, although it might not be in a manner you might expect. This is where being open and receptive to what comes serves you well. If you recall, one of the "Sacred Seven"— the Open and Willing Mind— was symbolized by

Your scene contains treasures that have significance to you. Your soul is talking to you in three-dimensional form.

a figure of a baby sitting on a stack of books and reading. He was completely open and willing to learn. Like that baby, look upon your tray scene and the miniatures in it as an opportunity to explore, discover and learn all sorts of new and wondrous things. Your scene contains treasures that have significance to you. Your soul is talking to you in three-dimensional form. When you do not allow the thinking mind to interrupt the organic and divine flow of conversation, the *knowing place* has full opportunity to share its knowledge.

2. Once you have fully explored the first miniature or cluster of miniatures you were drawn to, move on to the next one that catches your eye. Ask the same question, "What about this holds my attention?" Again write down whatever feelings and answers spontaneously come. Record the thoughts and feelings that surface WITHOUT JUDGEMENT and from a place of pure objective observation.

To understand more about the concept of being in the now, I recommend the book "The Power of Now" by Eckhart Tolle.

Acknowledge and be with what surfaces. Do not analyze, critique or think about what is happening. . .not at this time. This phase of the process is about being present and allowing whatever wants to be revealed, to do so. This is why having a means to document the journey is important. Later you will have an opportunity to think about what has occurred. For now, simply be present to the process. At this phase of the Sand Play experience being in the moment, fully receptive, without judgment, is essential.

3. When you have journeyed through your entire tray scene and you feel the exploration is complete, return to viewing your scene as a whole entity. Ask these questions: How does each miniature or cluster of miniatures relate to the others? How does the overall scene feel as a whole, now that I have explored each specific part?

This overview helps gather the specifics of your sand tray story into a unified whole. Our lives operate on many different levels of awareness and functioning, and the content of our stories have numerous components which encompass the whole of who we are. The Sand Play journey helps us to unravel and decipher the intricate code that makes up our entire human package. We are shedding the 'layers of the onion' so to speak and searching out the pieces that will help us solve the puzzle of our lives—including what is working well and what is out of kilter.

Sand Play shows us how to engage more fully in our lives in a healthy, happy and wholesome manner. It also assists us to address and resolve the difficulties—what is not working effectively in our lives. Individually speaking, or in a group setting, Sand Play explorations provides its participants with core information which brings into light the expanded version of who we are. . .that which seeks to unfold.

The more we inquire from a place of pure knowing—untainted by established belief systems or what we were taught to believe—the more we receive answers which reflect an accurate picture of who we are in relation to ourselves and the world in which we live.

The Final Phase

After the Sand Play process is finished take photos of your scene from different angles—and then step away. "Take a breather!" Allow some time and distance between you and your creation. For some, a few minutes may be all that is needed, for others it may take as long as a few days to integrate the experience. The saying that comes to mind is "What a difference a day makes."

A lot can happen in twenty-four hours. You may find that a great deal can happen in an hour or even minutes. So much can be revealed in one session of Sand Play. Although you have already done the facilitation and have received your initial feedback, reviewing your sand tray and what you have recorded offers further insights. Time and distance helps you to be fresh and clear when you look at or, literally, review the information again following the self-facilitation.

If a tremendous amount happened during your session and you had a life-transforming breakthrough, give yourself time to digest what occurred. Too much of a good thing can be overwhelming. It is important to allow yourself time to integrate this profound experience. Later, once your photos are developed, keep them with your recorded and dated information. (Also, when to disassemble your tray scene and put your treasures away is up to you. Some people may want to revisit their scene over a period of days. Others may feel complete shortly after the self-facilitation.)

When the process seems complete and you feel ready to move on to your next journey, ask yourself, "Am I done?" If you are uncertain, the chances are that you are not ready. If you receive a definite "Yes," consider that you are complete and ready to dismantle the scene.

Alternative Approaches to Doing Sand Play

Many people dialogue with their representations of The Divine or God through varying forms of sacred ritual such as prayer, chanting, meditation and so forth. They may utilize communication mediums of music, dance, art, and writing among other expressions. Sacred objects (items of deep and significant meaning to us) also serve to help us connect with The Divine Source. Often we display such objects in prominent places in our homes. Other ways we may connect with the All Knowing, All Encompassing include our interactions with other human beings, the living earth, animals. . .all that exists in our world, animate or inanimate. There are innumerous ways to open channels of communication with the *knowing place*.

Personal Sacred Altars

Personal Sacred Altars are sacred holding spaces for personal treasures of deep significance and meaning which are arranged in groupings varying in size. Altars are usually situated in a place of prominence, and often serve the mental, emotional or physical needs of a person, usually for spiritual, religious or other sacred reasons. In nearly every home I've visited, I have seen some variation of a sacred altar. People live with objects of meaning of innumerous shapes and forms everyday – some because of the profound significance they have in their lives, others because of their beauty and appearance.

Photos of loved ones, works of art, knick-knacks, keepsakes, treasures from the earth, bought or made gifts that touch us in some deep and heart-warming way. . .the list can go on indefinitely. In my home you will find rocks and crystals and other mementos from the natural earth, items hand-made, bought or gifted of deep sentimental value varying in shape and size. All sacred mementos are arranged in groupings to reflect, compliment and nourish the heart and soul of who I am and those important in my world. My studio also contains a number of specialty areas housing modified versions of sacred altars.

One alternative to doing *Sand Play for the Soul* is to create your own sacred personal altar. In many ways you may have already experienced alternative approaches to this form of expression, and may not have been aware. The difference now is you have the opportunity to do so with conscious intent. You can tune into another level of meaning and significance of your most cherished belongings through the self-facilitation process (mentioned earlier), with these objects as a symbolic reference point. The information you receive adds purposeful substance beneficial to your life if you allow it to do so.

In the next few paragraphs I will share examples of how I made use of sacred altars to offer you a framework as to how to create one for yourself. (You may already have a modified altar in your own home.) Sacred altars can assist you in opening up to "the highest and best in you", in powerful and revealing ways.

When my brother passed away at the age of forty-one, I took possession of some stuffed animals given to him by his friends, family, colleagues and clients as expressions of their love for him. Peter was a loving and generous person by nature and these people loved to gift him soft and cuddly animals. The furry creatures made a person smile by just looking at them. Symbolically they reflect who he was when he was alive. Those animal treasures are now at home in my studio in a sacred cluster sitting on three giant pillows. Many children and even some adults I have worked with have received solace and comfort from them. They have been given a life of their own by the minds and hearts of clients attracted to them.

There is one "being" in this particular sacred altar whom I call "Watch Puppy." He is a giant stuffed dog, who watches over those who play with him in my studio. In the story of "Physician Heal Thy Self," the physician, Len, received his special message from this giant gentle creature as he proceeded to hug this representation of cuddly, innocent love. The wisdom he heard was vital to his living with cancer. "Watch Puppy" loves to be hugged, and often serves as an additional player when my young clients and I play therapeutic board games.

In my living room resides a sacred altar on two hand-crafted shelves. On one shelf is a Bohemian crystal tray, hand-crafted by Czech master artist, surrounded by other beautiful crystal objects crafted by the same man. The crystal tray, in particular, is magnificent in its beauty and design, and deeply touches me emotionally every time I look at it. This and the other works of art came from my brother's estate. They are all dearly cherished treasures because when I look at them, I feel the beauty and exquisiteness of his being. The best in him is reflected in these in items. It rekindles in me a sense of elegance and original beauty.

Another sacred arrangement I have is on an end table consisting of a crystal rock with gold enclosures and some additional smaller gold rock pieces my father gave to me. These treasures came from thousands of feet below the earth's surface, a gift my dad brought back from his days as a miner. This crystal is absolutely beautiful! It reminds me of the profound connection my father has with the mineral kingdom. He talks with Mother Nature and listens to her responses. He often shares with me loving wisdoms from her heart and soul. As I look at this crystal, I feel its ancient power. It is used on occasion by clients in the sand tray, and almost always ends up in one of my self-made tray scene. When people tune into what it represents, after it finds its way into one of their sand trays, wondrous and revealing information is brought forth.

Walk around your house today and examine those keepsakes of special significance and meaning. If you were to tune into what specifically it is about those items that moves and touches you mentally, emotionally and physically, you may be delighted by what is revealed. To find meaning in your significant items refer to the Self-Facilitation section.

In the "Sacred Seven" chapter, I refer to the photo of my godchild's face nestled under her mother chin, so innocent and pure. This is another example of how an item in your home could awaken the best in you. When I view this picture my heart flutters. Purity and innocence awakens in me and I know all is right and beautiful in the world. When I'm feeling down, just looking at this picture helps me shift my attitude and choose another approach to looking at my life circumstances. It reminds me of all the innocent and joyful times when I am blessed to play with my godchild.

What thoughts and feelings are awakened in you when you tune in to a personal treasure in your home? What would happen if a number of those special items where placed together in one sacred grouping? Could the sacredness and significance of these pieces empower you to open up to insights and wisdom that could assist you on your journey in an expanding and uplifting manner? If so, in what way? It is a matter of choice and where we choose to place our attention.

Imagine finding various cherished items around the house, small enough for you to carry, and then placing them on an altar near your bed, in the bathroom, on your desk, or an area of a room you visit daily. Place them on a special cloth, on a favorite piece of furniture, on a kitchen counter or table. . .or put your treasures in a garden, or on a mat on the floor. A *Sand Play for the Soul* experience can be modified in a manner to compliment your needs, circumstances and desires.

Soul Dialogue through Journaling:

A powerful alternative to Sand Play is journaling. You can use 'objects of significance' to assist in the dialogue between you and your soul, or not, depending on your preference.

With objects of significance you can ask yourself the same kinds of questions as if you were facilitating your own Sand Play journey. The only difference is that you are exploring the significance of a cluster of miniatures you place and arrange in front of you on a surface, or in a holding space, that may be other than a tray filled with sand. If you choose to do this variation you still do a clearing and set the intent from your *knowing place* (as mentioned earlier) before gathering your treasures. Next, arrange them in front of you in whatever way you are spontaneously drawn. Begin your dialogue by allowing them to symbolically speak to you through words on paper. The self-facilitation questions for Sand Play apply here as well.

If you do not wish to work with 'objects of significance,' and feel the urge to write only, journaling is still an empowering way to help you release pain, frustration and negative emotions like anger and fear. Journalling also assists you to receive the clarity needed make decisions more easily; spark your creativity; uncover a bigger picture for your life; and reach new connections with your soul's voice. There does not need to be any rules. If anything emerges that criticizes or judges, take a deep relaxing breath and with the exhale release the mind chatter. Allow yourself to shift your energy from the head to heart as you would when doing Sand Play. In my experience, when we sit quietly with that open page before us the topics and questions that need to be addressed begin to emerge of their own accord. Then we have only to write them down and the self-exploration has begun.

You can do journaling almost anywhere. Materials used for journaling can range from a paper bag and a pencil to handmade papers and ultra deluxe pens. One friend's preference is an 11" by 13" sketchbook. She likes it because the surface of the paper is durable and she can use a variety of pens, glue things to it, draw with pastels, and even use light washes of watercolor to augment her writing. My own favorites change from time to time. My current preference is a smaller variety averaging 5" x 7" in size, nicely bound in cloth or leather with an antique feel to it. Feel free to explore a variety of different options to discover what kind of journal is right for you.

Sometimes we discover that in order to heal ourselves we must first seek to heal our inner child or adolescent self. Journaling gives us an opportunity to dialogue with these younger aspects of ourselves to discover what might yet need healing from those earlier years. If images of yourself at a younger age emerge while you are journaling, you may want to inquire about them by dialoguing with these images in your journal. Invite them to speak to you. Ask them if there is anything they want you to know about them that needs to be heard or expressed. . .perhaps something that could be helpful and healing for them and you. Whatever questions and answers surface, this is your sacred space to do what needs and wants to be done. And if invited, the Soul's *knowing place* will help guide you every step of the way.

"We work—and ideally we learn—to separate our own calls from the background noise. This is exactly why I began my own journal writing. . ."

The journal is also an excellent way to process unfinished business with others in our lives, even if they are no longer available to work with, person-to-person. You can even work in your journal with people who have died. Again, creating a dialogue with the person can bring about effective understanding of the problems we experienced with these people. Once we see and understand what happened with them, there is much more room for healing.

A significant use of journaling is to discover our own way—the actions that will heal us, that bring us joy and satisfaction in our lives, perhaps even the career or calling we may be seeking in which we can use our talents and abilities to benefit others. Gregg Levoy, author of Callings: Finding and Following an Authentic Life, says, "We work—and ideally we learn—to separate our own calls from the background noise. This is exactly why I began my own journal writing at the age of nineteen, and I have kept at it every year since."

The journal can be used to face our past and our present. A common tool for journaling is free association: you begin by writing a thought and just let the pen lead you from one thought to another without any effort to make sense. It is amazing what can be discovered in such an act. Another tool is to write a list of the problems in your life, even things you would rather run from than address, followed by a list of what is going well. Often creating such a contrast gives a starting point for further exploration and self-discovery.

Sometimes people have a difficult time getting started with journaling. This is usually because some adult told us that what we wrote was not good enough. Remember that your journal is for your eyes only—you do not need to share it with anyone else. It is your private place to explore not only the difficulties in your life, but new possibilities as well. The more you allow yourself to dream in your journal, the greater the possibility the dream will become your reality. In my experience, journaling is but one of many tools to help you change and grow. Use it when it's working for you, but you don't have use it all the time.

I invite you to explore this valuable tool of self-discovery and healing. Use it either alone, or in concert with other self-discovery techniques such as Sand Play, or Visual Journaling which you will learn about in the section that follows. Journaling is a powerful tool for self-disclosure and healing, especially if you allow it to be.

Soul Dialogue through Visual Journaling

Malieta Wise is a master in the craft of Visual Journaling. I have respect and appreciation of my colleague for the work she has done for clients we have mutually facilitated in our respective specialties. When they come to me for a Sand Play I often hear them comment with positive enthusiasm how much fun and benefit they received from her Visual Journaling class.

Visual Journaling in Malieta's Own Words

"The Visual Journal is a process of preparing a page in a journal with the use of paints, stamps, photos, or hand drawn images to set the stage for writing about something you have emotional content around. This can be a simple as tracing around your hand and writing about the gifts or road blocks you experience in your own life or as complicated as applying color and line in an abstract way and then letting these marks on the page guide you. You do not need to be an artist to do this.

"Often people may abort a part of what they may write because of the inner critic or because of a fear someone may read their deepest thoughts. Neither of these needs to be stopping points. If one is willing to be lead from the inside, feelings prompted by the image, a deep kind of intimate connection is possible. It often surprises, sometime amuses, and almost always proves beneficial to set some time aside to do this. I suggest this be done as needed—not daily—but with frequency to keep current with yourself. This will vary from person to person.

"A typical experience of this may be to make a mask, photograph it and insert the photo in the pages of your journal—adding a body if you wish. Be quiet for a time and really look at what you have created and then either write a dialogue with the face, have it speak to you, or simply describe the process of making it. Because it is from one's own hand, it is a kind of Shaman or Wise Person that can tell you more about yourself than most people expect.

"This and many other samples of exercises can and do, in my experience, call up a kind of primal wisdom that is always present— 'That Which' never leaves you, no matter what name you give this . . .'that' being our own best teachers. This two-way dialogue allows for a peace in the body and soul to foster truth and harmony. The reminder that we are much more than what we feel, comes full circle each time we engage in this activity. I have witnessed a major break-through in people who were stuck in some area of their life path—and often through their tears, a kind of deep joy seeing that it was by their own hand that this information was accessed."

About Malieta Wise

Malieta has worked in the field of expressive arts most of her adult life. Her studies flow from art education, studio art, philos-ophy, theology and early childhood education. For many years she conducted workshops with her husband Joe Wise, using art for healing in retreat and therapeutic settings. She began the Art Enrichment Program, a school program that allows schools to take part in art after school hours. Currently she teaches classes to adults and children in her community. She is a painter, printmaker, sculptor and member of several art organizations which she has been invited to speak. For more information on Visual Journaling, go to: www.joeandmalietwise.com.

Sand Play Safe Guards

You have decided to do *Sand Play for the Soul*. It feels right and safe to do so. You have taken the necessary basic steps outlined in the "how to" section of this book and you are ready. As you go on your journey if an uncomfortable, upsetting or disturbing, thought or feeling surfaces, do not fear. This is opportunity to become aware that something within you seeking to be acknowledged and healed. Below are some safeguards to use should this arise.

First remember, the intent has already been set. Your *knowing place* has been called into action to show you what you most need to know about your life at this time. Whatever may be surfacing may not be as upsetting or unsettling as it at first seems. When you allow yourself to learn the whole story you have more choice to respond and make decisions from a more informed place. I encourage you to refer to the story about Lilly "Operating from a Full Deck of Cards." Her state of terror dissipated as she explored the symbolism of objects that made her feel good and safe. The energy of fear quickly diffused because her strength and inner wisdom also was given a voice.

If you find yourself face to face with an emotional or mental challenge, take a deep relaxing breath and with each exhale release the tension, anxiety or fear from your body. Allow yourself to return to a state of acceptance and relaxation. After you feel a sense of calm returning to your body, ask your soul, "Who or what in my tray scene is loving, supporting and wise that can help me understand and deal with what is presently going on inside of me?" If there is no item in your tray that you are drawn to that can offer this knowing, ask if there is some other object in your home, or elsewhere, that can offer comfort and assistance to deal with what has come up for you to address.

Perhaps there is a spiritual or religious figure, or photo, that has brought you peace, comfort and insight in the past. It can be almost anything that has offered you strength, wisdom and understanding. It could be that you simply need to take a deep breath, look out into a garden, feel the sun upon your skin, hug a pet, or allow yourself to shed some tears. Maybe you just need to scream or express some aggression in your tray scene. Ten year old Ron, in the story "Ron and the Minion" released a lot of fear, anger and frustration by doing battle in his sand tray scenes, as did Jason in the story, "Jason and the Two Lizards." The sand tray is a very safe place to express whatever needs to be expressed, released and healed. It is far better to do so in the tray than on the outside where serious damage can be done to you or other people.

If these alternatives to calm the emotional/mental troubled waters do not work because a flashback from childhood, or an event once blocked from memory, has arisen and now feels overwhelming, I strongly encourage you to seek skilled, professional assistance to help you work through the situation. If necessary call 911. Other options to consider may be to seek support and guidance through prayer, meditation, and communion with whom or that which you turn to for

"Divine Intervention." I refer to this as "calling in the BIG GUYS" . . .all the healthy, supporting, powerful, loving, Divine forces available in existence. When I'm going through some mental, emotional, physical or spiritual challenge, I use all resources available to me.

Important Note: Doing Sand Play for yourself, as intended by this book, is designed to go on a fun, insightful, personally uplifting and expanding journey of self-discovery and realization. When the *knowing place* of your soul is guiding the sojourn in the sand tray, you will know by how good you feel: The process feels empowering and honoring of "the best in you."

The Soul Speaks and
Sets the Record Straight

"Wherever you go there I will be. You and I are woven from the same energy source. I assist when you ask for assistance, I love and support when you are ready and willing to allow the Divine into your life. I am but a humble servant whose sole purpose is to show the magnificence of who you are in the bigger picture of your life.

"Just say, 'Yes, I want to know who I am so that I may walk in life with my head held high, my arms spread in surrender, and my heart wide open to all that is good, loving and wondrous, being human on planet earth.'

"*Sand Play for the Soul* is an insightful, fun-filled, tangible way to dialogue with the Higher Knowing of Self. I enter into this realm of exploration in most surprising and pleasant ways. You have the opportunity to be privy to a communication tool capable of allowing you to move quickly and easily through your ever-changing life challenges. How something as simple as playing in a sand box could offer so much knowledge, support and assistance to a person may seem amazing to you yet how it works is really quite simple.

"Somewhere in the creation of life there is a source, an existence of energy that created us into being. This fact of life may seem boggling to the human mind. Whatever created you, the world, and existence, must be all-knowing and resourceful to do what it is does. You have been given Will, and what you do with that Will through choices you make, whether influenced by your belief system, or the outer world reality, affects what happens on your life journey. Whatever spiritual or religious beliefs you follow, one obvious truth remains steadfast: "That Which" caused you into being is omnipresent and omnipotent. It is this "All Powerful One" which gave form to the Soul and the *knowing place* in which it resides. I am one with you, if you allow me to awaken within you. Your willingness to dialogue with this expression of life is what allows Sand Play do what it is capable of doing. For the receptive and responsive participant the possibilities are infinite.

"Therefore. . .it is not doing Sand Play itself that is creating the phenomenal results, it is the individual choosing to dialogue with their soul in the *knowing place*, and this can take place regardless of setting or form.

"But I must now say in conclusion, it sure can be lots of fun dialoguing with me in the 'sand box' whether it be in the world in all its fullness, or a miniature version in a tray filled with sand. Come explore and discover with me and see for yourself how much we can accomplish in an hour of play."

-The Soul as experienced by Paula Petrovic, the Sand Play Lady-

Testimonials

Personal Testimonials

My five-year-old son's night terrors stopped immediately after his first sandplay session. By his fourth visit, his drawings of terrorizing monsters became mostly happy, not scary. He has power over his fears and himself and a confidence in himself he did not have before.

-Mother of Three Children, Sedona, AZ-

****

My brain tumor spoke loud and clear in my sand tray. It revealed to me what I needed to know. . .'Physician Heal Thyself.' I listened to my wiser self and did what needed to be done. Insights I received from my sand tray scene were invaluable. My tumor is dormant and I am living a healthy and full life.

-Dr. Len Levine, Physician/Surgeon, Ottawa, Canada and co-author
of *Open Minds: A New Perspective on Healing.*-

****

Sandplay was a wonder-full experience! At first it was fun, then suddenly it became serious, and I was healing non-verbally, very deeply. I highly recommend your process for children and adults.

- Erin M., School Psychologist, California -

****

Your Sand Play groups provided a very safe, fun environment for my daughters and son to go deeply in themselves. Through their sand tray scenes they released a lot of hurt, anger and frustration over my divorce with their father. I saw their souls speak. Years later I had a fifth child, who has been doing sand play with you since the age of eighteen months, and absolutely loves it.

- Terry Allen, Performing Artist and Mother of Five Children -

****

I had the opportunity to experience a Sandplay session facilitated by Paula early in Nov. 1995. At the time of the session, I personally had some troubling issues in my life that were causing me much stress.

What Sandplay did for me was to help clarify many feelings and decisions I knew I must make. Paula has a unique way of guiding you to reveal what your sub-conscious mind is telling you. The method of using a variety of small figures and toys seems to make it easier to create a visual image of your personal situation in a non-threatening, easy to understand way. Sandplay helped put focus back into my life.

- Paul Barton, Banker -

****

Clearly the work you did with me was profound. It brought my unconscious needs to the forefront and provided me with insight and empowerment for making decisions and changes in my life which supported further growth personally and professionally.

- Sophia Tarila, Ph.D., Author and Educator -

******

I have experienced many forms of growth work in the past, and have found the "sand play therapy" that we did together among the most powerful. I feel that sand play is one of the most gentle, subtle, and profound forms of inner healing work. Your skill at bringing forth sought after information is excellent.

-Gloria Reeder-

Business Testimonials

The purpose of this letter is to thank you for guiding me through the"Sandplay Exploration," which I found to be both profound and illuminating. The importance of this singular event has enabled me to clearly focus my intention and will into the growth of this corporation; and, your ability to create a safe environment for this experiential process to unfold is uncanny. I hope this recognition of your remarkable talent will in some measure provide you the recognition you so richly deserve.

- John Freedom, Operating Officer, Miracle Systems, Inc. -

******

"I want to offer congratulations on an idea whose time has come. Your "Sandplay" is not only fun but tremendously enlightening as well. The intrigue of using one's own tools for learning, combined with your ability to observe and assist clients in a non-threatening way to understand the symbolism of chosen items makes this process beneficial for any participant.

As an addition to the corporate environment, whether in a conference setting or in terms of retreats, I heartily recommend your program to other sponsors. Having had the opportunity to play a mini version myself, I can personally attest to it effectiveness in creating an awareness of current situations and internalized responses which are otherwise not consciously expressed. Please keep me posted on your progress. Best wishes for continued and growing success.

- Linda Chandler, International Consultant/Speaker/Trainer
to Fortune 500 Companies -

****

I wanted to take this opportunity to thank you for the lovely experience of the SandWorks session. It was certainly enjoyable and amazingly insightful. It confirmed many things which I knew were happening in my life and gave me many more important things to think about. I shall enjoy the photo of my sand tray scene forever. The world and its people need healing. SandWorks will help many people move into greater awareness of how to emotionally heal their wounds. The insights gained are powerful. I wish you great success on your continued journey.

- Dr. Heather Anne Harder, Author, Educator and Entrepreneur -

Workshop Testimonials

I was brought to a house, somewhere in Sedona, Arizona, and really had little sense of what was going to happen in my life. All I was told is that I was going to play in the sand. As I arrived, other people of different backgrounds began to show up. Once everyone arrived we sat quietly on the floor in the living room. Paula came in and explained a few things about what was about to happen and then asked everyone to pair off and step into "the sandbox room." I stepped into the room and looked around. Everyone was picking a box to sit by. Against the wall I saw a gentleman and felt that was where I belonged. I went over and introduced myself and we talked a bit.

Paula explained how the sand play worked. All of us were to pick from toys, knickknacks and other figurines around the room, separately, and then go back to our sandboxes and put a scene together. My first thought was this is silly. I wondered how this was going to help anyone.

But something happened during this sand play which was transforming. Even though my partner, Mike, and I didn't know anything about each other and picked our miniatures separately, and even worked in the sandbox separately, a picture was appearing that explained many things that were going on in both Mike's and my lives.

I was able to find meaning in things that I normally took for granted. Paula then worked with each group member and had everyone describe what type of metamorphosis took place for them. This became exhilarating and fun. I would recommend "sand play" with Paula for anyone who feels stuck in a void of life. It will awaken your spirit and make your heart happy.

- Lance Kulman -

There was a group of 16 or 17 of us and I paired off with someone I did not know. The four walls of Paula's studio were filled with shelves of miniatures. One could create a tray scene of any type because there were so many miniatures. It was like being a child again—even more fun.

I found my partner and I seemed to work easily without much need to define boundaries. This in and of itself was insightful because I like to work by myself. As we put together our tray and then explained it to Paula and other members of the group, I found myself understanding more about what I had been struggling with. The transformation from this understanding was so complete my partner and I did a second tray. It was much different and brought more insight.

I found Paula's sandplay to be an excellent way to process feelings and thoughts which caused me to be stuck in my life. Also, because it was like playing it is great fun. I highly recommend sandplay for anyone wishing to understand or process something going on in their life.

- Coralee Kulman -

****

As one of the facilitators for the Woman's Healing Retreat sponsored by Turtle Island Project, this is a letter to say thank you. Your program SandWorks: Powerful Tools for Creative Solutions, and expertise as a consultant and facilitator provided the women who attended the retreat with a truly unique and transformational experience.

Your work was inspirational, in that the participants experienced a deeper awareness and understanding of their own healing potentials and abilities to discover creative solutions to the core issues in their lives that needed to be addressed. Your inviting, playful, and energetic style allowed the women to safely explore delicate and personal issues in their lives with a sense of joy, discovery and personal reflection.

- Joyce C. Mills, PhD., Play Supervisor and Educator,
Author of: *Reconnecting to the Magic of Life* -

Recommended Reading

Bach, R., (1977). *Illusion: The Adventures of a Reluctant Messiah*. Dell Publishing, New York.

Canfield, J. & Hansen M. V. & Spilchuk B. (1996). *A Cup of Chicken Soup for the Soul*. Health Communications, Florida.

Gibran, K. (1951). *The Prophet*. Alfred A. Knoff, Inc. New York.

Levine, L., MD, DPH, CCFP, DAc. & Verspoor, R., et al. (2004). *Open Minds: A New Perspective on Healing*, Book Coach Press. Ottawa, Canada.

Mills, J.C., Ph.D., *Reconnecting to the Magic of Life*. Imaginal Press. Kauai, Hawaii

Tolle, E. (1999). *Power of Now: A Guide to Spiritual Enlightenment*. New World Library. Novato, California.

(continues...)

For those interested in knowing more about Sand Play from a clinical perspective:

De Domenico, G. S, Ph.D. *Sand Tray World Play: A Comprehensive Guide to the Use of Sand Tray in a Psychotherapeutic and Transformational Setting.* Vision Quest Images, 1946 Clemens Road, Oakland California.

Kalff, D.M (1995). *Sand Play: A Psychotherapeutic Approach to the Psyche.* (1980). Boston: Sigo Press.

Labovitz, B.B. & Goodwin E.A. (2000). *Sandplay Therapy: A Step-By-Step Manual for Psychotherapists of Diverse Orientations.* W.W. Norton & Company, Inc.

About the Author

Paula Petrovic's career spans over twenty-seven years and three continents. As a consultant, facilitator, educator, and counselor, she has worked with a wide range of age groups and populations. In private practice she works with the private, professional and business sectors facilitating individual and group sessions, workshops and retreats.

Her skills, talents and passions have empowered her clients from all walks of life to actualize their potential with clarity, enthausiam and success. Some of her greatest joys are Sand Play, writing, performance arts, traveling and playing in the inner and outer worlds of Life. If there is a heart-felt, soul-stirring discovery to experience Paula is present and eager to venture beyond limitation into New Worlds of Possibility.

To inquire about book signings or talks, or "Sand Play for the Soul" Advenutres, Workshops, Retreats, or Individual Sessions, you can write Paula at:

Paula Petrovic
c/o Soul House Press
P. O. Box 1541
Sedona, Arizona, 86339

or email her at Paula@SandWorks.net
or contact her through her website:

www.SandPlayfortheSoul.com or www. SandWorks.net

We invite you to share your feedback.

Printed in the United States
61345LVS00004B/202-258